WONDER THROUGH THE YEAR

A DAILY DEVOTIONAL FOR EVERY YEAR

WHITNEY HOPLER

Wonder Through the Year: A Daily Devotional for Every Year

First Edition. Copyright © 2024 by Whitney Hopler. The information contained in this book is the intellectual property of Whitney Hopler and is governed by United States and International copyright laws. All rights reserved. No part of this publication, either text or image, may be used for any purpose other than personal use. Therefore, reproduction, modification, storage in a retrieval system, or retransmission, in any form or by any means, electronic, mechanical, or otherwise, for reasons other than personal use, except for brief quotations for reviews or articles and promotions, is strictly prohibited without prior written permission by the publisher.

All Scripture quotations are taken from the Holy Bible, New International Version ®, NIV ®. Copyright © 1973, 1978, 1984, 2011 by Biblica, Inc. ™ Used by permission of Zondervan. All rights reserved worldwide. www.zondervan.com The "NIV" and "New International Version" are trademarks registered in the United States Patent and Trademark Office by Biblica, Inc. ™

Cover Design: Honor Hopler

Interior Design: Sarah Hamaker

Published by: Whitney Hopler, www.whitneyhopler.com

ISBN: 9798344568515

Nonfiction

❀ Created with Vellum

I dedicate this book to my wonderful readers and our wonderful God.

JANUARY

January 1st

As the new year begins, God's creation is revealed in the crisp winter air, inviting you to start fresh with a sense of wonder.

Pursue Wonder:
Step outside and breathe in the cold, fresh air. Let the chill awaken your senses and reflect on how God's creation renews itself. In what ways do you hope to find renewal as you start this new year?

Pray:
Dear God, thank you for the fresh start that each new year brings. Help me to embrace the wonder of your creation in the winter air and to begin this year with a renewed soul. Amen.

January 2nd

God can use dreams to reveal his plans and purposes, leading you toward your calling with clarity.

Pursue Wonder:
Ask God to speak through your dreams, revealing more about his plans for your life. Keep a journal of any recurring themes or symbols in your dreams, and seek God's guidance on what they might mean. Allow your dreams to deepen your understanding of your God-given purpose.

Pray:
Dear God, thank you for guiding me through dreams and revealing your plans for my life. Help me to discern your voice and follow the path you have set for me. Lead me with clarity and purpose as I seek to fulfill my calling. Amen.

January 3rd

The intricate patterns of frost on a window display God's artistry, showing the Creator's attention to detail in creation.

Pursue Wonder:
Look closely at the frost on a windowpane or outside. Marvel at the delicate designs and reflect on how God's creativity is evident in the smallest details of the world around you.

Pray:
Dear God, thank you for the beauty of your creation that I can see even in the patterns of frost. Help me to notice the details of your work and to appreciate the wonder of your artistry. Amen.

January 4th

God's love burns like a fire, providing warmth in the cold of winter.

Pursue Wonder:
Spend time by a fire or wrap yourself in a warm blanket today.

Reflect on how God's love is like the warmth that shelters you from the cold, bringing comfort to your soul.

Pray:

Dear God, thank you for the warmth of your love that surrounds me, especially during the cold winter months. Help me to feel your presence and to share that warmth with others. Amen.

January 5th

You can discover God's wonder through music, which opens your heart to God's presence with you.

Pursue Wonder:

Take time today to listen to a piece of music that stirs your soul – in any genre of music you enjoy. As you listen, let the melodies and harmonies remind you of God's creativity and the ways God orchestrates beauty in the world and in your life. Reflect on how music can be a prayer of praise, connecting your heart to God.

Pray:

Dear God, thank you for the gift of music that lifts my soul to you. Let the sounds of music draw me into a deeper awareness of your presence with me. Amen.

January 6th

Prayer isn't just about speaking to God; it's also about listening to God's voice. In the stillness of prayer, you can discover the wonder of God's presence in unexpected ways.

Pursue Wonder:

Today, take a moment to listen during your prayer time. After presenting your requests to God, sit quietly and ask him to speak to your heart. Let go of distractions and notice the peace that comes from simply being in God's presence. As you listen, you may hear God's voice in a new way.

Pray:

Dear God, please teach me to listen for your voice in prayer. Help me to quiet my thoughts and open my heart to receive the wonders of your wisdom and love. Amen.

January 7th

Snowflakes, which are each uniquely beautiful, put God's creativity and grace on display.

Pursue Wonder:

Look at pictures of different snowflake patterns online. Reflect on how each snowflake is unique, just as God's grace is uniquely tailored to each of us. If it's snowing where you live, take a few minutes to watch snowflakes fall from the sky like gifts from God.

Pray:

Dear God, thank you for the beauty of snowflakes that remind me of your beautiful and abundant grace. Help me to see your grace in my life and to extend it to others. Amen.

January 8th

You can find God's wonderful peace in the quiet of a winter morning, where the world seems to pause and breathe in God's stillness.

Pursue Wonder:
Wake up early and experience the stillness of a winter morning. Listen to the quiet and reflect on how God's peace fills your life, calming your soul and bringing stillness to your heart.

Pray:
Dear God, thank you for the quiet of winter mornings that bring calm to my soul. Help me to carry this peace with me throughout the day and to share it with others. Amen.

January 9th

God's timing is often different from your own timing, but trusting in God's perfect plan reveals the wonder of how God aligns circumstances according to his will.

Pursue Wonder:
Through prayer, you can learn patience and perseverance. Think

about a situation you've been praying about for a long time. Today, reaffirm your trust in God's timing, knowing that God's answers may come in unexpected ways. Reflect on how God has worked in the past, surprising you with his faithfulness. Trust that God will do so again.

Pray:
Dear God, help me remain steadfast in prayer, even when answers seem delayed. I trust in your perfect timing and the wonder of your plans for me. Please strengthen my faith and remind me that you are always at work. Amen.

January 10th

God's strength is like the ice that forms over a flowing stream, resilient and protecting what lies beneath.

Pursue Wonder:
If you can, watch a frozen stream or pond. Reflect on how the ice protects and preserves the water beneath, just as God's strength shields you and helps you endure life's challenges.

Pray:
Dear God, thank you for the strength that protects and sustains me, like the ice over a stream. Help me to trust in your strength and to rely on you in every situation. Amen.

January 11th

Celebrate God's gift of joy to you in the warm glow of candles – small lights that bring cheer to the darkest days of winter.

Pursue Wonder:

Light a candle and enjoy the warmth and light it brings to your space. Reflect on how even the smallest light can bring joy and how God's light shines in your life, dispelling darkness.

Pray:

Dear God, thank you for the light that brings joy to my life, even in the darkest days of winter. Help me to see your light in every situation and to carry that light to others. Amen.

January 12th

Dreams are a gift from God, and the Holy Spirit helps renew your mind as you deal with your thoughts and emotions during dreams.

Pursue Wonder:

Before going to bed tonight, pray and ask God to speak to you through your dreams. Keep a notebook by your bed to record any dreams you have upon waking. Pray about the details you remember, asking the Holy Spirit to show you the meaning of your dreams and how God wants you to respond to them.

Pray:

Dear God, thank you for speaking through dreams. Help me to be open to your messages as I sleep and to understand how you are leading me. May I always seek your wisdom and guidance in every aspect of my life. Amen.

January 13th

In a world filled with noise, silent meditation opens a sacred space for you to connect with the wonder of God's presence. As you meditate on God's Word, you can experience the depth of God's love and the peace that transcends understanding.

Pursue Wonder:
  Set aside a few minutes for silent meditation today. Focus on a short passage of scripture, such as Psalm 46:10: "Be still, and know that I am God." As you meditate on this verse, let its truth sink into your soul. In the silence, notice the wonder of God's nearby peaceful presence.

Pray:
  Dear God, help me to embrace silence as a way to experience your presence. May I find wonder in the stillness as I meditate on your Word and your goodness. Amen.

January 14th

The warmth of God's love can bring you comfort and joy during the chilly days of winter.

Pursue Wonder:

Enjoy a hot drink today, such as tea, coffee, or hot chocolate. Reflect on how this simple warmth can bring comfort to your body and soul, just as God's love brings warmth to your heart.

Pray:

Dear God, thank you for the comfort and warmth that a hot drink brings on a cold day. Help me to feel your love in the small pleasures of life and to share that love with others. Amen.

January 15th

God's strength can invigorate you with renewed energy and help you overcome challenges.

Pursue Wonder:

Step outside and take a deep breath of the cold, crisp air. Reflect on how the freshness of winter air can invigorate your body and mind, reminding you of the strength God gives you to face each day.

Pray:

Dear God, thank you for the invigorating air that fills my lungs and inspires me. Help me to draw on your strength as I face the challenges of this season. Amen.

January 16th

God's light shines through even the darkest seasons.

Pursue Wonder:

Step outside or look out your window and notice how the sunlight shines through the bare branches of trees in winter. If you have snow on the ground, notice how sunlight makes the snow sparkle. Reflect on how God's light shines through the darkest times, bringing hope in every season.

Pray:

Dear God, thank you for the beauty of sunlight on snow that reminds me of your constant light. Help me to see your light shining through every season of my life. Amen.

January 17th

Contemplative prayer – dwelling in God's presence without any agenda – allows you to experience the wonder of God's being. There is no rush, just an invitation to rest in the wonder of who God is.

Pursue Wonder:

Set aside time today for contemplative prayer. Focus on a simple phrase, such as "God is love," and let your heart and mind rest in that truth. As you slow down and simply be with God, notice the wonder of God's strong yet gentle presence surrounding you.

Pray:

Dear God, I come to you in quiet contemplation, simply resting in your love. Help me to experience the wonder of being still before you, knowing that you are always with me. Amen.

January 18th

God's love can flow into your life through family and friends as you enjoy the warmth of a shared meal together during the cold winter.

Pursue Wonder:
　　Share a warm meal with loved ones today. Reflect on how the warmth of good food and fellowship is a reflection of God's love, nourishing both body and soul.

Pray:
　　Dear God, thank you for the warmth of a shared meal and the joy of fellowship with loved ones. Help me to experience your love in these moments and to share it with others. Amen.

January 19th

When you pray for others, you participate in God's work of bringing grace, love, and healing into their lives. This intercession opens your heart to the wonder of how deeply we are all connected through God's love.

Pursue Wonder:
　　Spend time today in intercessory prayer, focusing on the needs of

others. As you lift them up to God, consider how God works through your prayers to impact lives, often in ways you may never see. This unseen power of prayer is a reminder of the depth and mystery of God's love for us all.

Pray:
 Dear God, thank you for the privilege of praying for others. As I pray, please send your love flowing through me into their lives. Show me how I can be a part of the wonder of your work in the lives of those I lift up today. Amen.

January 20th

When you enjoy a winter walk, each breath and step you take can remind you of God's gift of life to you.

Pursue Wonder:
 Take a walk in the winter air, feeling the cold against your face and the crunch of the frozen ground under your feet. Reflect on how each breath and step is a gift from God. Thank God for the joy of being alive.

Pray:
 Dear God, thank you for the gift of life and the joy that comes from experiencing your creation. Help me to find delight in the simple pleasures of this winter day and to appreciate each moment as a gift from you. Amen.

January 21st

The endurance and perseverance of winter athletes reflects the strength God gives to overcome challenges.

Pursue Wonder:
   Watch or participate in a winter sport like ice skating, skiing, or snowshoeing. Reflect on how the endurance required for these activities mirrors the strength God provides to help you overcome challenges in life.

Pray:
   Dear God, thank you for the strength and endurance you give me to face life's challenges. Help me to draw on your power and to persevere in faith, just as winter athletes endure their trials. Amen.

January 22nd

You can find God's peace in the soft glow of streetlights on a winter evening.

Pursue Wonder:
   Take a break to enjoy the soft glow of streetlights or outdoor lights this evening. If you have ice or snow in your area, notice how they reflect the lights. Reflect on how this peaceful scene brings calm to your mind as you rest from your work.

Pray:

Dear God, thank you for the calming beauty of a winter evening, when my day's work is done and I can rest in you. Help me to carry this peace with me and to find comfort in your presence. Amen.

January 23rd

When you bundle up for warmth in the cold, you can remember how God covers you with his protection and care.

Pursue Wonder:

As you bundle up in warm clothes today, reflect on how God provides for your needs and protects you from harm. Consider how God's love wraps around you like a cozy blanket, keeping you safe and warm.

Pray:

Dear God, thank you for your protection and care that surround me like warm clothing on a cold day. Help me to feel your love and to trust in your provision. Amen.

January 24th

When you pray with an expectant heart, you open yourself to the wonder of God's power and faithfulness.

Pursue Wonder:

As you pray today, approach God with confidence, knowing that he is listening and cares deeply about every detail of your life. God hears every prayer, and his answers are full of wisdom and love. Pray with expectation, trusting that God will answer in his perfect timing. Let the wonder of God's faithfulness fill your soul with hope.

Pray:
Dear God, I expect the best from you, and I trust in your goodness and power. Help me to experience the wonder of your answers as I seek your will in my prayers. Amen.

January 25th

Evergreen trees reflect God's constant strength as they stand tall and vibrant during winter.

Pursue Wonder:
Look at the evergreen trees around you, noticing how they remain strong even in the coldest weather. Reflect on how God gives you the strength to stand firm in your faith, no matter what challenges you face.

Pray:
Dear God, thank you for the strength that sustains me through every season, just as the evergreens stand firm in winter. Help me to remain steadfast in my faith and to draw on your strength in times of need. Amen.

January 26th

In the stillness of sleep, God can use your dreams to plant seeds of creativity and divine inspiration.

Pursue Wonder:
   Tonight, ask God to inspire your dreams with creativity and fresh ideas. When you wake up, take note of any images, ideas, or feelings that linger from your dreams. Consider how God may be speaking to you and inviting you to embrace new possibilities.

Pray:
   Dear God, thank you for the way you speak through dreams and inspire my heart. Help me to listen to your voice in the night and follow your direction with boldness. Amen.

January 27th

You can share God's love by helping a neighbor, and your kindness will bring warmth to both of you.

Pursue Wonder:
   Help a neighbor with a winter task, like shoveling snow or clearing ice. Reflect on how acts of service reflect God's love and bring warmth and connection to those around you.

Pray:

Dear God, thank you for the opportunities to share your love through acts of service. Help me to be a blessing to my neighbors and to spread your warmth in my community. Amen.

January 28th

The icy patterns that form on tree branches are each a delicate masterpiece of God's creation.

Pursue Wonder:
Take a close look at the ice on tree branches, noticing the intricate patterns and formations. Let yourself be inspired by how each detail is a testament to God's wonderful creativity.

Pray:
Dear God, thank you for the beauty of icy patterns that decorate the winter landscape. Help me to see the wonder of your creation in every detail and to appreciate the artistry of your work. Amen.

January 29th

Layers of snow that accumulate on the ground can remind you of God's wonderful strength that is constantly available to you.

Pursue Wonder:
Observe the layers of snow that have accumulated over time – either in person, if there's snow on the ground in your area, or by

looking at snow online. Reflect on how each layer adds to the strength and resilience of the earth, just as God's strength builds within you through each experience.

Pray:
   Dear God, thank you for the strength that grows within me, layer by layer, just as snow builds up over time. Help me to draw on this wonderful strength in difficult times and to trust you to keep empowering me when I need your help. Amen.

January 30th

The diversity of the people around you meet shows God's wonderful creativity at work.

Pursue Wonder:
   Spend time today noticing and appreciating the uniqueness of the people you encounter – friends, family members, colleagues, and even strangers. Consider how God has created each person with distinctive gifts, talents, and perspectives.

Pray:
   Dear God, thank you for the diversity of people you have placed in my life. Help me to appreciate the uniqueness in others and to see your image in everyone I meet. Teach me to value each person as you do. Amen.

January 31st

The wonder of a winter sunset can remind you God's constant presence with you.

Pursue Wonder:

Watch the sunset on this winter day, feeling the warmth of the fading light. Thank God that he is there with you at all times – even as the day ends – and tell him how much his constant presence means to you.

Pray:

Dear God, thank you for the warmth of a winter sunset that reminds me of your constant presence. Help me to feel your love in every moment of my life and to trust in your unchanging care. Amen.

FEBRUARY

February 1st

The simple act of focusing on your breath can draw you into a deeper awareness of God's presence. Through mindful breathing, you can experience the wonder of God's life-giving Spirit within you.

Pursue Wonder:
    Spend a few moments today focusing on your breath as a form of meditation. As you inhale, imagine breathing in God's peace and presence. As you exhale, release any stress or anxiety into God's care. This mindful breathing practice can help you feel grounded in God's love and experience God's wonder in a tangible way. If possible, do this outside in the cold winter air so you can see the steam from your exhaled breath in the air around you.

Pray:
    Dear God, please fill me with your peace as I breathe in your presence. Help me to release my worries and rest in the wonder of your love. Amen.

February 2nd

You can feel God's presence in moments of stillness, where quiet reflection opens your heart to God's voice.

Pursue Wonder:
    Find a quiet place today, either indoors or outdoors, and spend a few minutes in stillness. Reflect on how these moments of quiet allow

you to hear God's gentle whispers and feel God's presence more deeply.

Pray:

Dear God, thank you for the gift of stillness, where I can hear your voice and feel your presence. Help me to seek out these quiet moments and to listen closely to what you have to say to me. Amen.

February 3rd

You can share God's kindness in the small gestures you offer to others.

Pursue Wonder:

Make a warm drink like coffee, tea, or hot chocolate and share it with a friend or family member. Reflect on how small acts of kindness can warm the hearts of others, just as God's kindness warms your soul.

Pray:

Dear God, thank you for the warmth that comes from small acts of kindness. Help me to share your love with others through simple gestures that bring comfort and joy. Amen.

February 4th

You can experience joy from God by taking a wonder walk in winter, where the crisp air and serene landscape invite you to slow down and pay attention to the wonder around you.

Pursue Wonder:

Take a winter wonder walk today, feeling the crisp air on your face and noticing the stillness of the season. Reflect on how this quiet time outdoors allows you to connect with God and experience joy in the beauty of creation.

Pray:

Dear God, thank you for the joy of exploring your creation, even during winter. As I walk, let me feel your loving presence with me. Amen.

FEBRUARY 5TH

You can recognize God's wisdom in the natural rhythms of life, where rest and renewal are essential for growth.

Pursue Wonder:

Take some time to rest and recharge today, embracing the natural rhythm of work and rest that God has established. Reflect on how this balance is key to living a healthy and fulfilling life.

Pray:

Dear God, thank you for the rhythms of life that remind me of the importance of rest and renewal. Help me to honor these rhythms and to trust in your wisdom as I seek balance in my daily life. Amen.

February 6th

The bright colors of winter berries against the snowy landscape reveals God's creativity even during dreary winter days.

Pursue Wonder:
   Look for winter berries or other vibrant colors in the landscape today. Reflect on how God's creativity brings beauty to every season, adding color and life where you might least expect it.

Pray:
   Dear God, thank you for the beauty of winter berries that bring color and life to the cold landscape. Help me to see the vibrant ways you are at work in my life, even in difficult seasons. Amen.

February 7th

You can see God's creativity reflected in the art that inspires your soul, drawing you closer to God.

Pursue Wonder:
   Admire a work of art today that moves you. Reflect on how creativity is a gift from God, meant to draw you closer to God's beauty and truth.

Pray:
Dear God, thank you for the gift of art that inspires me. Help me to see you at work in every creative expression and to be inspired by the beauty that points back to you. Amen.

February 8th

Baking on a winter day fills your home with a fragrance that can remind you of God's kindness.

Pursue Wonder:
Spend time baking something warm and delicious today, such as fresh bread or cookies. As the aroma fills your home, consider how God's kindness brings warmth and comfort to your life, nourishing both your body and your soul.

Pray:
Dear God, thank you for the simple joys of baking and the warmth it brings to my home. Help me to savor these moments and to share your kindness with others through acts of generosity and care. Amen.

February 9th

You can experience God's love when gathering with friends and family, enjoying conversation and laughter together.

Pursue Wonder:

Invite friends or family over for a cozy gathering, or plan a way to meet virtually if you can't be together in person. Reflect on how these connections warm your heart and remind you of God's love in your life.

Pray:

Dear God, thank you for the warmth that comes from gathering with loved ones. Help me to cherish these connections and to see your love reflected in the relationships I hold dear. Amen.

February 10th

You can experience God's kindness through the warmth of hospitality, where sharing your home with others can make them feel valued and loved.

Pursue Wonder:

Invite someone who needs your encouragement over to your home today to talk. Reflect on how simple acts of kindness, like opening your home to enjoy a conversation with someone, can demonstrate God's love.

Pray:

Dear God, thank you for the warm connections that come from sharing my home with others. Help me to offer my hospitality generously, and let your love flow through me as I do so. Amen.

FEBRUARY 11TH

Enjoying a meal together with a friend or family member can remind you of how God nourishes you in many wonderful ways.

Pursue Wonder:
　　Share a meal with someone today, at home or at a favorite restaurant. Let your senses delight in the wonderful tastes and scents of the food. Enjoy how the act of sharing food brings you closer to others and to God, nourishing both your body and your soul.

Pray:
　　Dear God, thank you for the blessing of shared meals that nourish both body and soul. Help me to enjoy these experiences fully with the people I love. Amen.

FEBRUARY 12TH

You can experience God's love in the joy of shared laughter that lightens your hearts and strengthens your bonds.

Pursue Wonder:
　　Spend time with friends or family today, and enjoy some humor that makes you all laugh. Thank God for the joy and connections your experience in your relationships.

Pray:

Dear God, thank you for the gift of laughter I can share with the people I love. Help me to find joy in every day and to share that joy with those around me. Amen.

February 13th

God's kindness flows through you as you care for others, like offering a warm scarf or gloves to someone in need on a cold winter day.

Pursue Wonder:
Find a way to offer warmth to someone in need today, such as by donating winter clothing to a local charity or helping a neighbor. Consider how acts of kindness, no matter how small, reflect God's wondrous care for all people.

Pray:
Dear God, thank you for the opportunities to show kindness to others. Help me to be your hands and feet, sharing your love with those around me. Amen.

February 14th

God's love is at the heart of Valentine's Day, and you can celebrate that God is the source of all love you experience every day.

Pursue Wonder:
Celebrate all forms of love today – romantic love, friendship, acts

of kindness, and more. Thank God for the wondrous love he gives you and calls you to share with the world.

Pray:
Dear God, thank you for the gift of love that you have poured into my life. Help me to celebrate this love today and to share it with others in ways that reflect your heart. Amen.

February 15th

You can experience God's wonder in the power of words, where thoughtful conversations and kind affirmations encourage people.

Pursue Wonder:
Make an effort today to engage in a meaningful conversation with someone you want to encourage. Consider how the words you speak feature great power to help people if you use them well.

Pray:
Dear God, thank you for the wonderful gift of words and the power they hold to encourage people. Help me to use my words wisely and lovingly, reflecting your kindness and truth to those around me. Amen.

February 16th

You can see God's grace in moments of forgiveness, where relationships are restored and hearts are made whole.

Pursue Wonder:

Decide today to forgive someone who hurt you, or to seek forgiveness from someone you have hurt. Thank God that his grace empowers you to find peace and repair relationships.

Pray:

Dear God, thank you for the power of forgiveness that restores and heals. Help me to give your grace to others and to seek reconciliation in my relationships. Amen.

February 17th

You can experience God's wonder when you learn something new by reading a good book.

Pursue Wonder:

Settle down with a good book today, allowing yourself to get lost in its pages. Discover something new from what you read, and let that inspire you.

Pray:

Dear God, thank you for the simple pleasure of reading and for all the wonderful new information I can learn from books. Amen.

February 18th

You can experience the wonder of God's love by hugging someone you care about and appreciate.

Pursue Wonder:
　Give or receive a hug today, feeling the warmth and connection it brings. Thank God for how his love flows between you and the person you're hugging.

Pray:
　Dear God, thank you for the gift of physical touch that helps me experience and share your love. Remind me to hug the people I love often. Amen.

February 19th

You can experience God's creativity in the variety of flavors and foods that nourish your body and bring joy to your senses.

Pursue Wonder:
　Try a new recipe or savor a favorite meal today, appreciating the flavors and textures. Reflect on how God's creativity is expressed in the diversity of foods that nourish and delight you.

Pray:
　Dear God, thank you for the abundance and variety of foods that

you provide to nourish my body and delight my senses. Help me to be mindful of your provision and to share what I have with others. Amen.

February 20th

God's love will flow through your life into someone else's life when you send a handwritten note or card, offering words of encouragement to someone who needs it.

Pursue Wonder:
　　Write a note or card to someone who could use encouragement today. Reflect on how your words can be a source of kindness and love, just as God's Word brings comfort and hope to your life.

Pray:
　　Dear God, thank you for the power of words to uplift and encourage. Help me to use my words to share your kindness and love with others, offering hope and comfort where it's needed most. Amen.

February 21st

God's love is like the warmth of the sun breaking through the winter clouds, bringing light and hope to the coldest days.

Pursue Wonder:
　　Step outside today and feel the warmth of the sun on your face,

even if it's just for a moment. Reflect on how God's love breaks through the clouds of life, bringing hope and joy to your heart.

Pray:

Dear God, thank you for the warmth of the sun that breaks through the winter clouds. Help me to feel your love shining in my life, even on the coldest and darkest days. Amen.

February 22nd

Look for God's wonder in the simplicity of winter branches that are bare yet full of promise, waiting for the new life of spring.

Pursue Wonder:

Observe the bare branches of trees today, seeing the beauty in their simplicity. Reflect on how these branches, though bare, are full of promise – just as God's promises are always faithful and true.

Pray:

Dear God, thank you for the beauty of winter branches that remind me of the promise of new life. Help me to trust in your promises and to see the beauty in every season of life. Amen.

February 23rd

You can feel God's love in the kindness you share with others, as it reflects God's love flowing through you.

Pursue Wonder:

Reach out to someone today with a simple act of kindness, such as sending an encouraging text or helping someone with a small task. As you do, reflect on how your kindness is a reflection of God's love in the world.

Pray:

Dear God, help me to reflect your kindness in my actions today. May my small gestures of love point others to you and remind me of your presence. Amen.

February 24th

Dreams can be a way for God to remind you of his wonderful love for you.

Pursue Wonder:

At bedtime tonight, pray about the ways you need God's love in your life. As you sleep, allow your heart to be open to the comfort of God's presence in your dreams. When you wake, spend time in prayer, asking God – the source of all love – to bring more love into any areas of your life where you need it. Trust that God is with you, even while you sleep.

Pray:

Dear God, thank you for your wonderful love that reaches me even in my dreams. Help me to trust you in every situation, knowing that your love is always available to me. Speak to me in the night and fill my heart with your love. Amen.

February 25th

God is always present, even in your pain. Lamenting through prayer allows you to be honest with God and welcomes God's wonderful comfort and healing into your life.

Pursue Wonder: Today, take time to bring your sorrows, worries, and grief to God in prayer. Rather than hiding from your pain, express it fully to God. Notice how, in the act of lament, God can reveal his presence to you in new ways, offering you peace that surpasses understanding.

Pray: Dear God, I bring my sorrow to you, knowing that you listen and care. Meet me in my pain and heal my heart. Please show me your goodness even in the hardest moments. Thank you; amen.

February 26th

God's kindness surrounds you like the warmth of a winter coat, giving you protection and comfort against the cold.

Pursue Wonder:
Put on your warmest coat today and take a moment to appreciate the protection it offers. Reflect on how God's kindness surrounds you like this coat, keeping you safe and secure in his love.

Pray:

Dear God, thank you for the warmth and comfort that your kindness provides. Help me to feel your protection in my life and to trust in your care, no matter what circumstances I face. Amen.

February 27th

God's love is like the wonderful warmth of a fire that is constantly burning in your life.

Pursue Wonder:
Gather around a fireplace or heater with loved ones today, enjoying the warmth and togetherness it brings. Consider how you can always rely on God's love to be there for you all.

Pray:
Dear God, thank you that your love is a powerful fire that always burns bright in my life. I love you. Amen.

February 28th

You can see God's wonder in the changing seasons, where winter's end brings the promise of spring and new life.

Pursue Wonder:
As February comes to a close, reflect on the changing seasons and the promise of new life that spring brings. Consider how God's

beauty is evident in the cycles of nature, where each season has its own unique wonder.

Pray:
Dear God, thank you for the beauty of the changing seasons, where winter gives way to the promise of spring. Help me to see the wonder in every season of life and to trust in your plan for my journey. Amen.

February 29th (Leap Year)

God's blessings overflow, filling your life with abundance and joy.

Pursue Wonder:
Reflect on the blessings in your life and how they overflow. Thank God for the abundant blessings he is constantly pouring into your life.

Pray:
Dear God, thank you for your overflowing blessings. Fill my heart with gratitude and help me to share your abundance with others. Amen.

MARCH

March 1st

Every part of nature reveals glimpses of God's wonder in some way.

Pursue Wonder:
Spend time in nature today and notice one detail that especially inspires you. What does it reveal to you about its Creator? Take photos or draw pictures of what inspires you, so you can enjoy looking at it later.

Pray:
Dear God, thank you that I can learn something about you from everything you've made in nature. Open my eyes to see your work in the world around me. Amen.

March 2nd

God meets your needs with perfect timing.

Pursue Wonder:
Reflect on a time when God provided for you in a surprising way. Share this testimony with someone to encourage his or her faith.

Pray:
Dear God, thank you for meeting my needs with perfect timing. Help me to trust in your provision and to share your faithfulness with others. Amen.

March 3rd

You can experience God's wonder through the creativity God has placed within you, using your gifts to reflect God's own divine creativity.

Pursue Wonder:
 Take time today to do a creative activity – cooking, gardening, playing music, drawing, writing, or something else creative that you enjoy. As you express yourself creatively, remember that you are made in the image of God, the Creator. When you create something beautiful, no matter how small, God's creative power flows through you. Consider how God can use the results of your creative gifts.

Pray:
 Dear God, thank you for the gift of creativity that you've placed within me. Help me to use my talents to reflect your beauty and bring glory to you. May my work today honor the creativity you've woven into every aspect of my life. Amen.

March 4th

You can experience wonder by noticing the changing winds that remind you of the Holy Spirit's movement in your life.

Pursue Wonder:
 Spend a few moments outside feeling the wind on your face. Reflect on how the wind, though invisible, moves with power – just

like the Holy Spirit in your life. Trust that even in unseen ways, God is always working to guide and shape your journey.

Pray:
　　Dear God, thank you for moving in my life through your Holy Spirit, even when I can't see or understand your work. Help me to trust your guidance as I deal with the winds of change. Amen.

March 5th

You can discover God's presence through wondrous music.

Pursue Wonder:
　　Listen to a worship song that resonates with you. Pay attention to how the music makes you feel – joyful, peaceful, reflective, etc. Let the music draw you closer to God, since it has the power to bypass words and connect directly with your soul.

Pray:
　　Dear God, thank you for the gift of music that speaks to my heart. Let it remind me of your wonderful presence with me. Amen.

March 6th

The wonder of God's perfect peace is available anytime and anywhere you connect with God.

Pursue Wonder:

Create a quiet space in your home today. Spend time there, meditating on God's peace and allowing it to fill your heart.

Pray:

Dear God, thank you for being my refuge from this stressful world. Fill my heart with the wonder of your perfect peace and help me to rest in your presence. Amen.

March 7th

God's light dispels darkness, bringing you clarity and truth.

Pursue Wonder:

Light a candle and reflect on how God's light brings clarity and truth to your life. Pray for areas where you need God's illumination in your life.

Pray:

Dear God, thank you for being the Light of the World, who dispels darkness in this fallen world. Please illuminate the areas of my life where I need your guidance. Amen.

March 8th

You can see God's wonder in water, which refreshes and sustains life just as the Holy Spirit refreshes your soul.

Pursue Wonder:

Take time today to drink a glass of water slowly or pause near a river, lake, or even a fountain. Reflect on how water refreshes your body and nourishes the earth, and how God's Spirit refreshes your soul in the same way. Let the simplicity of water remind you of God's constant provision for you.

Pray:

Dear God, thank you for the gift of water that refreshes and sustains life. Let me be reminded of how your Spirit nourishes my soul and fills me with life. Amen.

March 9th

You can witness the wonder of God's abundance through food, which reminds you of God's provision and care.

Pursue Wonder:

As you prepare and enjoy a meal today, take time to savor each bite. Reflect on how God provides for your physical needs with abundance, and how God cares for your soul with the same generosity. Let this simple act of mindful eating remind you of God's sustaining love.

Pray:

Dear God, thank you for the food that nourishes my body and the love that nourishes my soul. Help me to remember your provision at every meal. Amen.

March 10th

God's wonderful truth sets you free, liberating you from bondage and lies.

Pursue Wonder:
Identify a lie you've believed about yourself and replace it with God's truth. Consider how this truth brings more freedom in your life.

Pray:
Dear God, thank you for your truth that sets me free. Help me to reject lies and to embrace the freedom I can find in my relationship with you. Amen.

March 11th

God's wonderful patience is infinite, giving you time to grow and change.

Pursue Wonder:
Be patient with yourself today as you work on personal growth. Remember that God's patience gives you the space to change.

Pray:
Dear God, thank you for your infinite patience with me. Please

help me to be patient with myself and others as we grow and change. Amen.

March 12th

God's wonderful presence is your constant companion.

Pursue Wonder:
Spend a few moments in silence, simply acknowledging God's presence with you. Let God's love fill your heart and give you confidence.

Pray:
Dear God, thank you for your constant companionship. Please fill my heart with the assurance of your presence and help me to feel your love. Amen.

March 13th

God's wonderful love transforms you from the inside out.

Pursue Wonder:
Reflect on how God's love has transformed you. Share your story with someone who needs encouragement.

Pray:

Dear God, thank you for the power of your love to change me. Help me to share my story and to encourage others with the evidence of your work in my life. Amen.

March 14th

God's wonderful compassion for you can inspire you to care for others.

Pursue Wonder:
Show compassion to someone in need today through an act of kindness that helps meet that person's needs.

Pray:
Dear God, thank you for your wonderful care for me. Inspire me to show compassion to others and to be a reflection of your love. Amen.

March 15th

God's wonderful Word powerfully speaks love and truth to you.

Pursue Wonder:
Memorize a Bible verse or passage today. Let its powerful words speak love and truth to your soul.

Pray:

Dear God, thank you for the active power of your Word. Help me to memorize and meditate on it, allowing it to transform my heart and mind regularly. Amen.

March 16th

God's wonderful forgiveness is complete, wiping away your sins and making you new.

Pursue Wonder:
Confess a sin in your life to God, turn away from it, and ask God to forgive you for it once and for all. Thank God for wiping away your sin and making you new.

Pray:
Dear God, thank you for your complete forgiveness that makes me new. Help me to live in the freedom of your grace and to extend forgiveness to others. Amen.

March 17th

God's wonderful wisdom is a treasure, offering you the guidance you need to make the best decisions.

Pursue Wonder:
Seek wisdom from God for a decision you need to make. Write

down any insights you receive and take any actions God leads you to take.

Pray:
Dear God, thank you for the treasure of your wisdom. Guide my decisions and help me to seek your wisdom in all situations. Amen.

March 18th

God's wonderful goodness is abundant, overflowing in your life.

Pursue Wonder:
Take note of specific reasons why you're grateful today. Make a list of blessings and thank God for his abundant goodness.

Pray:
Dear God, thank you for the abundance of your goodness in my life. Help me to see and appreciate the blessings you provide each day. Amen.

March 19th

God's wonderful power is unmatched, even making miracles happen.

Pursue Wonder:

Recall a miracle you have witnessed or heard about, and consider how it demonstrates God's unmatched power.

Pray:
Dear God, thank you for the miracles that demonstrate your wondrous power. Help me to remember your power and to trust in your ability to do the impossible. Amen.

March 20th

God's creation renews as spring arrives, reminding you of God's power to bring new life.

Pursue Wonder:
Take a walk outside and notice the subtle signs of new life – buds on trees, birds singing, or the warmth of the sun. As the earth wakes up from winter, reflect on how God is renewing your heart and mind, bringing new growth into your spiritual life.

Pray:
Dear God, thank you for the gift of spring and how it reminds me that you are always renewing my spirit. Help me to embrace the fresh start you offer today. Amen.

March 21st

God's wonderful patience is unending, giving you time to grow.

Pursue Wonder:

Think about an area of your life where you need to grow. Thank God for his patience and ask for his help to make good progress.

Pray:

Dear God, thank you that there is no end to your patience. Help me to grow spiritually in the ways I need to, while relying on your grace and guidance. Amen.

March 22nd

God's wonderful joy is contagious, spreading hope in every situation.

Pursue Wonder:

Share a joyful moment with someone today by connecting with God together. Talk about the difference between joy (a strength you feel whenever you pay attention to God's loving presence with you) and happiness (an emotion you can feel only in good circumstances).

Pray:

Dear God, thank you for the gift of joy that I can experience in all circumstances when I connect with you and enjoy your presence with me. Help me to encourage others who need to experience the joy you make possible. Amen.

March 23rd

God's wonderful love is sacrificial, giving everything for your redemption.

Pursue Wonder:
Reflect on the ultimate sacrifice of Jesus on the cross. Spend time in prayer, thanking Jesus for his redeeming love.

Pray:
Dear God, thank you for the ultimate sacrifice of Jesus for my redemption. Fill my heart with gratitude for your love and help me to live in response to it. Amen.

March 24th

God's wonderful grace is unconditional, offering you favor you don't deserve.

Pursue Wonder:
Think about a time when you received something you didn't deserve. Thank God for how his unmerited grace has blessed your life.

Pray:
Dear God, thank you for your unmerited favor. Help me to recognize and appreciate the grace you freely give, and to extend grace to others. Amen.

March 25th

God's wonderful mercy has no limits.

Pursue Wonder:
Show mercy to someone today who may not deserve it, as a way to thank God for how his compassionate mercy has impacted your life.

Pray:
Dear God, thank you for your compassionate mercy. Help me to be merciful to others by being unconditionally kind, and to reflect your loving nature. Amen.

March 26th

God's wonderful faithfulness is a constant presence in your life.

Pursue Wonder:
Think about a time when you experienced God's faithfulness in a way that inspired you with awe. Share the story of this experience with someone who needs encouragement.

Pray:
Dear God, thank you for your constant presence in my life. Help me to trust in your faithfulness and to encourage others with my testimony. Amen.

March 27th

God's wonderful wisdom is infinite, guiding you well in every situation.

Pursue Wonder:
    Seek God's wisdom in a situation where you feel uncertain and need to make an important decision. Trust that God's guidance will lead you in the right direction.

Pray:
    Dear God, thank you for your infinite wisdom. Guide me in my uncertainty and help me to trust in your perfect direction. Amen.

March 28th

God's wonderful love is unconditional, accepting you just as you are.

Pursue Wonder:
    Reflect on how God has accepted you and loves you unconditionally. Thank God by showing unconditional love to someone else today.

Pray:
    Dear God, thank you for accepting me just as I am. Help me to reflect your unconditional love to others and to accept them as you do. Amen.

March 29th

God's wonderful generosity is unlimited, and God provides for you abundantly.

Pursue Wonder:
Give generously to someone in need today, out of gratitude for how God has provided for you.

Pray:
Dear God, thank you for your unlimited provision. Help me to give generously to others and to trust in your abundant care. Amen.

March 30th

God's wonderful peace is comforting, calming your fears.

Pursue Wonder:
Find a quiet place to sit and pray, inviting God's comforting peace into your heart. Enjoy experiencing how God's peace calms your fears.

Pray:
Dear God, thank you for calming my fears. I give my worries to you and ask you to intervene in every situation I'm concerned about, to do what's best. Please fill my heart with your perfect peace and help me to trust you to work in all of those situations. Amen.

MARCH 31ST

God's wonderful presence is powerful, transforming your life with his love.

Pursue Wonder:
Spend time in prayer, inviting God's powerful presence into your life. Reflect on how God's love has transformed you.

Pray:
Dear God, thank you for the power of your transforming love. Fill my life with your presence and help me to be a reflection of your love to others. Amen.

APRIL

April 1st

God's wonderful joy brings laughter into your life.

Pursue Wonder:
    Share a joke or a funny story with someone today. Enjoy experiencing how laughter is a gift from a joyful God.

Pray:
    Dear God, thank you for the gift of laughter. Please fill my heart with your joy and help me to spread joy to others. Amen.

April 2nd

God's wonderful Word is alive and active, guiding you in truth and wisdom.

Pursue Wonder:
    Spend time reading a passage from the Bible today. Reflect on how God's living Word speaks to you personally.

Pray:
    Dear God, thank you for the truth and wisdom I find in the Bible. Open my heart and mind perceive your messages to me and to respond to them faithfully. Amen.

April 3rd

You can feel God's presence in the warmth of the spring sun that reminds you of God's light.

Pursue Wonder:
   Sit outside and feel the warmth of the sun on your face. Reflect on how God's light and warmth are always with you.

Pray:
   Dear God, thank you for the warmth of the spring sun that reminds me of your bright presence. Let your wondrous light shine on me and guide my steps. Amen.

April 4th

God's creation is bursting with new life in the spring, reflecting God's wonderful creative power.

Pursue Wonder:
   Plant a seed or a flower today. Reflect on the miracle of growth and new life that God brings each spring.

Pray:
   Dear God, thank you for the new life and growth that spring brings. Help me to see your creative power in every part of creation and to appreciate the beauty of your work. Amen.

April 5th

Praise opens the door to God's wonder. When you focus on who God is – his love, holiness, and power – you shift your attention from earthly concerns to God's wondrous presence.

Pursue Wonder:
Spend time today in prayer solely focused on praising God for who he is. Don't ask for anything, but instead celebrate his goodness, love, and faithfulness. As you lift your praises, you'll notice how it draws you closer to God's wonder.

Pray:
Dear God, I praise you for your wonderful love, holiness, and power. Help me to stand in awe of who you are, letting praise open my heart to the wonders you reveal every day. Amen.

April 6th

You can see God's wonderful faithfulness through the changing seasons.

Pursue Wonder:
Reflect on the transition from winter to spring and how it demonstrates God's faithfulness. Thank God for being faithful and reliable in your life.

Pray:

Dear God, thank you for the changing seasons that remind me of your reliability. Help me to trust in your faithfulness and to see the wonder of your reliable work in my life. Amen.

April 7th

God's grace is like the gentle spring rain, refreshing and renewing your spirit.

Pursue Wonder:

If it rains today, take a moment to stand outside and feel the raindrops. If it doesn't rain, take a shower and feel how the water energizes you. Reflect on how God's grace refreshes and renews your spirit.

Pray:

Dear God, thank you for the gentle rain that refreshes the earth and my spirit. Shower me with your grace and renew my heart today. Amen.

April 8th

The budding trees that promise new beginnings can remind you of the hope God always offers you.

Pursue Wonder:

Notice the budding trees outside and consider the hope they represent. Think about new beginnings in your own life and how God's hope sustains you.

Pray:
Dear God, thank you for the promise of new beginnings I see in the budding trees. Please fill my heart with hope and help me to trust in your plans for my future. Amen.

April 9th

The vibrant colors of spring display God's wonderful creativity.

Pursue Wonder:
Take a walk and enjoy the vibrant colors of spring. Let the colorful beauty of God's creation during spring inspire you to trust God to give you creative ideas in your life.

Pray:
Dear God, thank you for the vibrant colors of spring that display your creativity. Open my eyes to see your creative work in the world around me. Amen.

April 10th

Tall trees can inspire you to trust God's protection, wisdom, and strength.

Pursue Wonder:

Spend time today near a tall tree – in your backyard, or along your street, or in a park. Notice its height, its branches reaching toward the sky, and its roots deeply anchored in the earth. Reflect on how trees are a symbol of God's protection and wisdom, offering shade and stability in all seasons. Like a tree, God's presence surrounds you with strength and security.

Pray:

Dear God, thank you for the beauty of trees that remind me of your wisdom and protection. Help me to root myself in your love and trust in your shelter. Amen.

April 11th

A gentle spring breeze can inspire to you to seek God's peace for your heart and mind.

Pursue Wonder:

Find a quiet place to sit and feel the gentle spring breeze. Ask God to send you the peace that only he can give you, to calm your heart and mind.

Pray:

Dear God, thank you for the calming presence of the gentle breeze. Please fill my heart with your peace and help me to rest in your care. Amen.

April 12th

The growth of new plants can remind you of God's renewing power.

Pursue Wonder:
Notice the new growth in plants around you. Ask God to renew your hope and energy today.

Pray:
Dear God, thank you for the new growth in plants that symbolizes your renewal. Please renew me in all the ways I need to be renewed, so I can grow in your love. Amen.

April 13th

You can find wonder in the simplicity of food, which sustains your body and reminds you of God's daily provision.

Pursue Wonder:
Today, prepare a simple meal with gratitude. As you gather your ingredients and cook, think about where the food came from – the soil, the sun, the rain – and how God orchestrates all of nature to provide for your needs. Eating is a holy act when you recognize God's provision in each bite. Let this moment remind you of how deeply God cares for you.

Pray:

Dear God, thank you for the food that nourishes my body and the love that sustains my soul. Help me to remember your provision in all that I do and eat today. Amen.

April 14th

You can experience God's wonder in the miracle of growth, where even the smallest seeds hold the potential for great transformation.

Pursue Wonder:
　Plant a seed today – in your garden, in a pot indoors, or simply in your imagination. As you cover it with soil, reflect on how God brings growth in unseen ways. Just as seeds transform into something beautiful with time and care, God works in your life in wonderful ways – often quietly, yet powerfully. Trust God to nurture your dreams and bring them to fruition.

Pray:
　Dear God, thank you for the wonders of nature that remind me of your transforming power. Help me to trust in your timing as you bring beauty and purpose to my life. Amen.

April 15th

God's promises are like spring flowers, bringing beauty and hope to your life.

Pursue Wonder:

Enjoy the new spring flowers around you. Reflect on God's promises and how they bring beauty and hope to your life.

Pray:

Dear God, thank you for the beauty of spring flowers that remind me of your promises. Fill my heart with hope and help me to trust that you will accomplish beautiful purposes out of even the most challenging situations I'm facing. Amen.

April 16th

The gentle and nurturing spring rain can remind you of God's wonderful kindness.

Pursue Wonder:

If it rains today, experience and appreciate the nurturing effect of the rain. If it's not raining today where you live, take a break to watch a brief video of gentle rain falling. As you watch the rain either in person or virtually, consider how God's kindness nurtures your soul.

Pray:

Dear God, thank you for the gentle rain that nurtures the earth and inspires my soul. Help me to see your kindness in the small moments of life, and to spread your kindness by choosing kind words and actions every day. Amen.

April 17th

God's faithfulness is a solid rock – a strong foundation in every situation.

Pursue Wonder:

Find a rock and hold it as you pray, reminding yourself of God's firm faithfulness. Reflect on how God is a completely reliable foundation for your life.

Pray:

Dear God, thank you for being my solid rock in all circumstances. Strengthen my faith and help me to rely on your unchanging nature. Amen.

April 18th

You can experience God's wonder through laughter, which refreshes your spirit and brings light to the world around you.

Pursue Wonder:

Today, make time for something that makes you laugh, such as playing with a pet or watching a funny show. Allow yourself to experience the lightness and freedom that come from enjoying humor.

Pray:

Dear God, thank you for the gift of laughter that lightens me up and refreshes my soul. Help me to find joy in simple moments and to share that joy with others today. Amen.

April 19th

The wonder of meditating on Jesus is that he is always present and always available to guide you.

Pursue Wonder:
Centering your meditation practices on Jesus can transform your day by helping you experience his love, grace, and wisdom in a personal way. Choose to meditate on an aspect of Jesus' character today. For example, focus on Jesus' compassion by reflecting on stories where he healed the sick or fed the hungry. As you meditate, feel the wonder of Jesus' compassion in your own life, and let it inspire you to show compassion to others.

Pray:
Dear Jesus, help me to focus on you in my meditation today. May I experience the wonder of your love and compassion, and may it overflow into the way I live. Amen.

April 20th

The slow growth of plants teaches us about the wonder of waiting for God's timing.

Pursue Wonder:
Watch the growth of a plant over time. Reflect on how God's patience is teaching you to wait on God's timing.

Pray:

Dear God, thank you for teaching me to wait on your timing through the slow growth of plants. Help me to trust in your perfect timing and to be patient when I need to wait. Amen.

April 21st

The resilience of nature reveals God's wonderful strength that is always available to help you.

Pursue Wonder:

Notice how nature recovers and thrives after a storm. Reflect on how God's strength helps you overcome challenges in your life.

Pray:

Dear God, thank you for the resilience of nature that reveals your strength. Help me to rely on your strength to overcome the challenges I face. Amen.

April 22nd

On this Earth Day, you can see God's wonder in the intricate design of the natural world, which reflects God's glory and creativity.

Pursue Wonder:

Take time today to care for the earth, such as by planting something or picking up litter. Consider how all of creation points to

God's qualities as the Creator. As you care for the environment, you honor God and help yourself and everyone else on our planet.

Pray:
Dear God, thank you for the beauty and diversity of nature. Help me to be a good steward of the earth you've entrusted to me and to recognize your wonderful work in every aspect of creation. Amen.

April 23rd

You can feel God's peace in the stillness of a spring morning.

Pursue Wonder:
Wake up early and spend some quiet time outside on this spring morning. Reflect on how the stillness brings peace to your soul.

Pray:
Dear God, thank you for the stillness of a spring morning that calms my spirit. Help me to seek your peace throughout my day. Amen.

April 24th

The wonderful songs of birds can inspire you by reflecting God's creativity and joy.

Pursue Wonder:

Listen to the birds singing today. Enjoy how their God-given songs inspire you.

Pray:

Dear God, thank you for the songs of birds that inspire me. Help me to find joy in the simple pleasures of life and to share that joy with others. Amen.

April 25th

You can see God's wondrous provision in blooming fruit trees that promise a generous harvest to come.

Pursue Wonder:

Walk by fruit trees that have flowers now, which show that they will produce fruit later this year. Consider how God's provision promises abundant nourishment in your life.

Pray:

Dear God, thank you for the blooming fruit trees that remind me of your generous provision for me. Help me to trust in you and to be grateful for the blessings you provide. Amen.

April 26th

Each individual spring flower is a masterpiece that displays God's wonderful creativity.

Pursue Wonder:
Take time to enjoy the variety of spring flowers around you. Reflect on how each one is a unique masterpiece of God's creativity.

Pray:
Dear God, thank you for the variety of spring flowers that display your creativity. Help me to appreciate the uniqueness of your creation and to see the beauty in diversity. Amen.

April 27th

The new growth of spring can remind you of God's compassion that offers you hope and renewal.

Pursue Wonder:
Notice the new growth of plants and trees around you. Consider how God's compassion offers hope and renewal in your life.

Pray:
Dear God, thank you for the new growth of spring that reflects your compassion. Please fill me with hope and renew my spirit with your love. Amen.

April 28th

The harmony and order of nature reflects God's wise design.

Pursue Wonder:
Pay attention to the harmonious and orderly balance of nature around you. Reflect on how God's wisdom creates harmony and order in your life.

Pray:
Dear God, thank you for the balance of nature that reflects your wisdom. Help me to seek harmony and order in my life and to trust in your wise guidance. Amen.

April 29th

God's kindness is like the gentle touch of a spring breeze, comforting and soothing your soul.

Pursue Wonder:
Feel the gentle spring breeze on your skin. Reflect on how God's kindness comforts and soothes your soul.

Pray:
Dear God, thank you for the gentle touch of a spring breeze that comforts my soul. Help me to feel your kindness in the small moments of life and to share that kindness with others. Amen.

April 30th

You can experience God's wonder through rest, as God invites you to slow down and find peace in his presence.

Pursue Wonder:

Today, set aside intentional time for rest and reflection. In the busyness of life, God calls you to embrace rest as an act of trust and surrender. Take a quiet walk, read quietly, meditate, or simply sit still. Use this time to realign your heart with God. As you rest, let God's peace wash over you, and know that in stillness, you can experience the wondrous depth of God's love and care for you.

Pray:

Dear God, thank you for the gift of rest. Please help me to slow down and focus on you. I trust that you are working even when I'm still. Amen.

MAY

May 1st

You can discover God's wonder in new beginnings, since each day offers a fresh start filled with grace and opportunity.

Pursue Wonder:
    As a new month begins, reflect on the new beginnings God provides in your life. God's mercies are new every morning, and today is a chance to embrace the fresh opportunities God places before you. Whether it's starting a new project, building a habit, or nurturing a relationship, invite God into this new season. Trust that God is guiding you and will make all things new in his perfect time.

Pray:
    Dear God, thank you for the fresh start you give me today. Help me to embrace this new month with hope and faith, trusting that you are leading me into the good plans you have prepared. Amen.

May 2nd

You can experience God's wonder through music, which lifts your spirit and connects your heart to God's heart in worship.

Pursue Wonder:
    Today, set aside time to listen to or play music that inspires you in any genre. Let the sounds resonate in your soul. Music is a powerful gift from God – a universal language that expresses emotions beyond

words. As you listen to music today, invite the Holy Spirit to move in your heart, drawing you closer to God through the beauty of sound.

Pray:
Dear God, thank you for the gift of music, which inspires me in ways that go beyond words. Let the music I hear today draw me closer to you. Amen.

May 3rd

The cycles of planting and harvest reveal God's wisdom by teaching lessons of patience and trust.

Pursue Wonder:
Plant a seed or tend to your garden today, if you can. Or, buy some fresh vegetables to eat. Reflect on how the cycles of planting and harvest teach us patience and trust in God's timing.

Pray:
Dear God, thank you for the lessons of planting and harvest that teach me patience and trust. Help me to rely on the wonder of your perfect timing in all areas of my life. Amen.

May 4th

You can experience God's wonder through the changing colors of the sky, as each sunrise and sunset points to God's artistry and faithfulness.

Pursue Wonder:
    Take time today to watch the sunrise or sunset. Notice the colors – the wondrous shades of gold, orange, pink, blue, and purple that fill the sky. Think about how each day begins and ends with God's creative touch, reminding you of his faithfulness. As you watch the sky transform, let it remind you that God is with you through every season of life, painting beauty into your life as you go through changes.

Pray:
    Dear God, thank you for the wondrous beauty of the sky, which reminds me of your creativity and constant care. As I watch the colors of the sunrise and sunset, help me to remember your goodness and faithfulness in my life. Amen.

May 5th

You can experience God's wonder through storytelling, where you recognize how God has been at work in the stories of your life and the lives of others.

Pursue Wonder:
    Reflect on the power of stories today, such as through reading a book, hearing someone's testimony, or sharing your own story. God is the ulti-

mate storyteller, as he weaves together the events of your life for good. As you listen to or tell a story, be mindful of the lessons, growth, and ways God has shown up. Consider how your own life is part of a much bigger story that God is writing, full of purpose and guided by love.

Pray:
Dear God, thank you for weaving together the details of my life into a beautiful story. Help me to see how you have been working in my story and to honor the stories of others, knowing that we are all part of your greater story. Amen.

May 6th

You can see God's faithfulness reflected in the return of migratory birds, as they remind you of God's care throughout all seasons.

Pursue Wonder:
Watch migratory birds return to your local area. Let their faithful journey inspire you to trust in God's wonderful care for you throughout every season of your life.

Pray:
Dear God, thank you for the return of migratory birds that remind me of your constant care. Help me to trust in your constant presence and guidance in my life. Amen.

May 7th

You can experience God's wonder through the power of the wind, which reminds you of God's unseen presence that moves and shapes the world around you.

Pursue Wonder:
Today, take a moment to feel the wind around you – whether it's a soft breeze or a stronger gust. The Bible often uses the wind as a metaphor for God's Spirit, moving in ways that you can't always see but can feel. Let the wind remind you of the Holy Spirit's work in your life, gently guiding and empowering you in ways beyond your understanding. Reflect on how God is always present, even when you can't see him, moving in your life like the wind.

Pray:
Dear God, thank you for the presence of your Spirit that moves like the wind, shaping and guiding my life. Please help me to trust in the unseen work you are doing and to remain open to your guidance every day. Amen.

May 8th

You can discover God's wonder in moments of quiet, where God's voice becomes clearer in the quiet stillness of your heart.

Pursue Wonder:
Seek out some quiet time today, in nature or in a quiet room. In that quiet environment, quiet your thoughts and listen for God's voice. Quiet can often be where God speaks the loudest, inviting you to rest and hear his guidance. As you sit quietly, let go of distractions

and anxieties, and allow yourself to simply be in God's presence, trusting that God is close to you.

Pray:

Dear God, thank you for the gift of quiet, where I can hear your voice more clearly. Help me to set aside noisy distractions, to embrace quiet, and to trust that in the quiet, you are speaking to my heart. Amen.

May 9th

You can experience God's wonder by sharing life with others, embracing the beauty of community as a gift that reflects God's relational nature.

Pursue Wonder:

Today, take time to intentionally connect with people around you – friends, family, work colleagues, and even strangers. Plan a meal, join a gathering, or engage in conversation with the purpose of building deeper relationships. God created us to live in community. As you open your heart to others, notice how God works through these connections, revealing the wonder of his love through shared experiences.

Pray:

Dear God, thank you for the gift of community. Help me to see your wonder in the people around me and to cherish the connections you've placed in my life. May I reflect your love through meaningful relationships. Amen.

May 10th

You can see the wonder of God's renewal as new green leaves show up on trees.

Pursue Wonder:
Notice the new green leaves that have appeared this spring on the trees around you. Consider how God's renewal brings new beginnings to your life.

Pray:
Dear God, thank you for how the new green leaves on trees bring new beginnings to mind. Help me to embrace the renewal you offer and to start each day fresh by connecting with you in prayer and meditation. Amen.

May 11th

You can discover God's wonder in the cycles of growth, where God's design for renewal is reflected in both nature and in your relationship with him.

Pursue Wonder:
Notice the stages of growth around you in nature on this spring day. Just as nature has seasons of growth, rest, and renewal, so do you. Reflect on the ways God has been growing you, even in the quiet or difficult seasons. Embrace the process of change with the confidence

that God is continuously at work, shaping you and nurturing your spiritual maturity.

Pray:
God of growth, thank you for the cycles of renewal you've designed, both in nature and in my own life. Help me to trust the process of growth, knowing that you are always at work, guiding me closer to you. Amen.

May 12th

God's grace blooms abundantly, like spring flowers do.

Pursue Wonder:
Spend time in a flower garden or park, enjoying the abundance of blooming flowers. Celebrate how God's generous grace brings beauty into your life.

Pray:
Dear God, thank you for the abundant grace you constantly pour into my life. Let blooming spring flowers remind me of your grace and inspire me to be graceful others. Amen.

May 13th

You can experience God's wonder in the gift of fresh food, which not only sustains your body but also nourishes your soul.

Pursue Wonder:

Today, enjoy some fresh spring produce – such as strawberries or leafy greens. As you savor each bite, reflect on how God provides for your physical and spiritual needs. Just as food sustains your body, God's presence nourishes your soul. Give thanks for God's provision in all areas of your life.

Pray:

Dear God, thank you for the gift of fresh food and for meeting all of my needs. Help me to see the wonder of your extraordinary work in the ordinary moments of my life. Amen.

May 14th

The companionship of animals, with their unconditional love and simple joy, points to God's wonderful care for all creation.

Pursue Wonder:

If you have pets or encounter animals today, take a moment to appreciate their companionship. Animals often demonstrate a sense of trust, loyalty, and joy that can remind you of God's unconditional love. As you interact with them, reflect on how God cares for all of his creatures – including you. Whether you're watching birds in your yard or playing with a pet, see this as a reflection of God's loving care for all life.

Pray:

Dear God, thank you for the gift of animals and their companionship. Help me to see your love reflected in the way they trust and love unconditionally, reminding me of your constant care for me. Amen.

May 15th

The warmth of the sun this month reminds you of God's steadfast love, which shines on you and brings life.

Pursue Wonder:
Spend a few minutes basking in the sunlight today. Feel the warmth on your skin and reflect on how God's love shines constantly, bringing light to your soul. Just as the sun is essential for you physically, God's love is essential for you spiritually.

Pray:
Dear God, thank you for the warmth of the sun and for the constant reminder of your love that never fades. Let your love shine in my life today, bringing light and life to all that I do. Amen.

May 16th

You can witness God's wonder through the fruit of the Spirit, as the Holy Spirit transforms you from within to reflect God's character.

Pursue Wonder:
Focus today on one of the fruits of the Spirit – love, joy, peace, patience, kindness, goodness, faithfulness, gentleness, or self-control.

Choose to intentionally cultivate this fruit in your interactions and actions today. As you allow the Holy Spirit to work through you, notice how you experience God's transformative power in real time, helping you grow in holiness. Each small act of love or patience reveals the wonder of God at work within you.

Pray:
　　Dear God, thank you for the spiritual fruit you are growing in me. Help me to cultivate them today, so my life will reflect your love and wonder to those around me. Amen.

May 17th

Dreams can be a powerful reminder of God's presence and an opportunity to engage with him in a deeper way.

Pursue Wonder:
　　Tonight, invite God to be part of your dreams. Before sleeping, spend time in prayer, asking God to reveal more of his presence to you in the night. As you sleep, be open to God's voice, comfort, and guidance. When you wake, reflect on how God might have spoken to you through your dreams, even in subtle ways. Trust that God is always close to you.

Pray:
　　Dear God, I invite you into my dreams. Speak to me, guide me, and comfort me in the night, and help me to recognize your presence when I wake up. May my dreams be a space where I encounter your love and peace. Amen.

May 18th

God's love is constantly faithful, like the cycle of seasons.

Pursue Wonder:
    Reflect on the constant cycle of the seasons and how it mirrors God's unchanging love. Thank God for his wonderful faithfulness in all seasons of life.

Pray:
    Dear God, thank you for the constant cycle of seasons that reminds me of your unchanging love. Help me to trust in your faithfulness through all the seasons of my life. Amen.

May 19th

When you see plants slowly growing, you can learn about the wonder of waiting on God's timing.

Pursue Wonder:
    Watch the growth of a plant over time. Let that inspire you to be patient and wait on God's timing for the answers to your prayers.

Pray:
    Dear God, thank you that your timing is perfect as you work in every situation I bring before you in prayer. Please help me to trust in your timing and to be patient in my journey. Amen.

May 20th

You can find God's wonder in the rhythm of the seasons, as each season offers new lessons and opportunities for growth.

Pursue Wonder:
Reflect on the changes that late spring brings, such as longer days, warmer temperatures, and the promise of summer ahead. Think about the different seasons of your life and how God has been with you through each one. Just as spring brings new growth, trust that God is always at work, bringing something new into your life.

Pray:
Dear God, thank you for the rhythm of life and the lessons you teach me in every season. Help me to embrace the growth and change you bring, trusting in your perfect timing. Amen.

May 21st

You can find wonder in the sweet scent of spring blossoms, which remind you of God's fragrance of grace and love.

Pursue Wonder:
Take a deep breath today when you encounter the fragrance of spring flowers like lilacs, roses, or gardenias. As you inhale their sweet scent, reflect on how God's grace permeates every part of your life, bringing joy and peace. Just as the flowers' fragrance lingers, God's love surrounds you each day.

Pray:

Dear God, thank you for the fragrance of your love that surrounds me like the scent of spring flowers. May I carry your grace with me wherever I go today. Amen.

May 22nd

You can feel God's peace in the stillness of a spring morning that calms your spirit.

Pursue Wonder:

Wake up early and spend a quiet moment outside this morning. Enjoy how the stillness brings peace to your spirit.

Pray:

Dear God, thank you for the stillness of a spring morning that calms my spirit. Help me to seek your peace in every part of my day. Amen.

May 23rd

You can discover God's wonder in the practice of grounding (earthing), where the earth beneath your feet reconnects you with God's creation.

Pursue Wonder:

Try grounding (also called earthing) today by walking barefoot on grass, soil, or sand. As you feel the earth's energy beneath your feet, remember that God formed you from the dust of the earth and designed you to live in harmony with his creation. Grounding has both physical and spiritual benefits, helping you feel more connected to the natural world and to the Creator who made it. Let this simple practice remind you of the stability and strength you can find in God.

Pray:
Dear God, thank you for the earth beneath my feet and the way it connects me to your creation. As I walk barefoot, help me feel grounded in your love and mindful of the world you've made. Amen.

May 24th

You can experience God's wonder through the warmth of the sun as it reminds you of God's constant light and presence in your life.

Pursue Wonder:
Step outside and soak in the sunshine today. As you feel the sun's warmth on your skin, reflect on how God's light brings life to everything it touches. The sun's rays nourish plants, warm the earth, and give you energy. Let this moment in the sun remind you that God's presence is always with you, offering warmth and guidance. Give thanks for the blessing of light, and be mindful of how God's light shines in your heart.

Pray:
Dear God, thank you for the gift of sunshine and the way it nour-

ishes all life. Help me to embrace your light today and allow it to fill my heart with your warmth and love. Amen.

May 25th

You can experience God's wonder in the vibrant skies of late spring, where the interplay of light and clouds reveals God's creativity.

Pursue Wonder:
    Take a wonder break today to watch the sky. Notice the constantly changing beauty above you – dramatic clouds, a clear expanse of blue, or the soft colors of a sunset. The sky is a daily masterpiece, reflecting God's vast creativity. Late spring often brings brilliant sunsets and dynamic cloud formations, so take time to enjoy these moments and be reminded of God's presence and infinite power.

Pray:
    Dear God, thank you for the beauty of the skies that reflect your glory. Help me to pause and appreciate the wonder of your creation today and every day. Amen.

May 26th

You can experience God's wonder through your God-given creativity.

Pursue Wonder:

Enjoy a creative activity today – cooking, writing, building, drawing, playing music, or working on another creative project. As you work, reflect on how God, the ultimate Creator, designed the entire universe with intentionality and love. Your creativity is a reflection of being made in God's image. Don't worry about perfection. Instead, focus on the joy of creating. Let the process remind you that God delights in your uniqueness and the talents he has given you.

Pray:
Dear God, thank you for allowing me to reflect your image through my creativity. Help me to embrace the joy of creating and use the creative gifts you've given me well. Amen.

May 27th

You can encounter God's wonder through the power of gratitude, which transforms your perspective and deepens your joy.

Pursue Wonder:
Make a list of 10 blessings you're grateful for today. As you write them down, let gratitude change your perspective on the day. Gratitude is a powerful way to experience God's presence and shift your focus from your challenges to your blessings. Take time to thank God for each item on your list, and notice how expressing thanks invites more joy and wonder into your life.

Pray:
Dear God, thank you for the many blessings in my life. Every-

thing I have is ultimately a gift from you. Help me to develop a heart of gratitude that brings me closer to you. Amen.

May 28th

You can experience God's wonder through the sensation of cool water that reminds you of God's refreshment and renewal for your soul.

Pursue Wonder:
　　Today, spend time in water. If you can, go swimming in a pool, lake, or ocean. If you can't go swimming, take a shower or bath. As you immerse yourself in water, reflect on the refreshment and cleansing that water provides, symbolizing the spiritual renewal God offers you. Let the coolness of the water remind you of how God refreshes your spirit, washing away stress and filling you with peace.

Pray:
　　Dear God, thank you for the gift of water and the way it refreshes and renews. Just as water revives my body, please refresh my soul and draw me deeper into your presence today. Amen.

May 29th

The animals and birds you see – which are each a unique part of God's creation – show you the wonder of God's creativity and care.

Pursue Wonder:

Take time today to watch the animals and birds around you, such as a bird flying overhead, a squirrel darting through trees, or a pet in your home. Notice how each creature reflects God's creativity and care for his creation. Consider how God's attention to detail in the natural world reflects God's attentiveness to your life.

Pray:
Dear God, thank you for the beauty and diversity of animals and for the way they remind me of your care for all of creation. Help me to trust in your care for me as well, since you are always watching over me. Amen.

May 30th

You can experience God's wonder when you prioritize your time in ways that align with God's purposes, opening space in your schedule for rest, reflection, and meaningful connections.

Pursue Wonder:
Take a few minutes today to reflect on how you're spending your time. Are you rushing through your days, or do you make space for moments of rest, reflection, and connection with God and others? Time is a gift from God, and managing it well allows you to experience more of God's presence. Choose one area of your life – morning, afternoon, or evening – and plan time for prayer, to connect with God intentionally during that time.

Pray:
Dear God, please help me to use my time wisely. Give me the

grace to slow down and make space for you in my daily life, so I won't miss the wonder of what you're doing. May I learn to see time as a gift and use it to draw closer to you. Amen.

May 31st

You can discover God's wonder in the balance of work and rest.

Pursue Wonder:

As you approach the end of the month, reflect on how you've been balancing work and rest. Have you been overburdened, or have you found time for restoration? God designed rhythms of work and rest so you can be replenished both physically and spiritually. Plan time today to recharge in a way that works best for you, such as taking a wonder walk, eating a meal mindfully, or spending a few extra minutes in prayer. By doing so, you'll find that rest is not a luxury but an important way to experience God's provision and care.

Pray:

Dear God, thank you for the balance of work and rest. Help me to recognize when it's time to pause and recharge, knowing that rest is part of your design for my life. May I experience your peace in those moments of renewal. Amen.

JUNE

June 1st

God's light shines brightly in the long days of June, illuminating your path.

Pursue Wonder:
　　Spend time outside during the long daylight hours. Reflect on how God's light illuminates your path and guides your steps.

Pray:
　　Dear God, thank you for the long days of June that illuminate my path. Help me to walk in your light and to trust in your guidance every day. Amen.

June 2nd

You can see God's wonderful provision in the growth of gardens and crops that promise a bountiful harvest later on.

Pursue Wonder:
　　Visit a garden or farm and notice how the plants are growing. Reflect on how God's generous provision for you promises a bountiful harvest in your life, as well.

Pray:
　　Dear God, thank you for always growing something good in my

life. Please help me to trust in your provision and to be grateful for your blessings. Amen.

June 3rd

You can see God's wondrous beauty reflected in the clear blue skies of summer that remind you of God's infinite creation.

Pursue Wonder:
   Look up at the clear blue sky and reflect on its vastness. Give thanks for how God's creation is infinite and beautiful.

Pray:
   Dear God, thank you for the beauty of clear blue skies that remind me of your infinite creation. Help me to appreciate the vastness and beauty of the world you have made. Amen.

June 4th

The gentle rustling of the wind through leaves can inspire you to slow down and pay more attention to the wonder of God's presence with you.

Pursue Wonder:
   Sit quietly under a tree and listen to the rustling leaves. Enjoy how this calms and clears your mind, so you can notice God's gentle yet powerful presence with you.

Pray:

Dear God, thank you for bringing peace to my soul. Remind me to rest in your presence whenever I need to connect with you more. Amen.

June 5th

The laughter of children playing outside can help you discover the God-given gift of joy.

Pursue Wonder:

Listen to the laughter of children playing outside on this summer day. Consider how their joy inspires you to be joyful, as well.

Pray:

Dear God, thank you for letting me enjoy children's laughter. Help me to embrace joy myself and to share it with others whenever I can. Amen.

June 6th

You can experience God's wonder in the rhythm of water's currents and waves, which reflect God's power and constancy.

Pursue Wonder:

Today, visit a river, lake, or ocean if you can. Take some time to sit and watch the currents and waves in the water. Notice how they move in a steady rhythm, just as God's presence remains constant in your life. Even if you're not near the water, you can still reflect on its powerful beauty through videos, sounds, or memories. As you see the currents and waves move through the water, let remind you of how God's love continually washes over you, renewing your soul.

Pray:
Dear God, thank you for the beauty and power of water in motion. Help me to feel your love flow over me like water currents and waves, bringing renewal into my life. Amen.

June 7th

You can discover God's wonder by taking a wonder walk with the specific purpose of seeking inspiration.

Pursue Wonder:
Today, take a summer "wonder walk" – a walk where you intentionally look for something awe-inspiring around you. As you walk, ask God to help you see his work in new ways. Pay attention to small blessings: the intricate design of a leaf, the sound of birds, or the way light filters through trees. Let this be a time to connect with God's creation and refresh your soul. When you return, thank God for the wonder you discovered.

Pray:
Dear God, as I walk today, help me to be open to the wonder of your presence in creation. Please show me something that reveals

your goodness and grace, inspiring me to feel awe. May I be more aware of how you are constantly at work around me. Amen.

June 8th

You can witness God's wonder in the intricate details of insects and small creatures, since each one is a testament to God's creativity and care.

Pursue Wonder:
Today, spend time observing small creatures like ants, bees, or butterflies. Watch how they move, work, and interact with their surroundings. These tiny beings reflect God's meticulous attention to details. Whether it's the industriousness of an ant or the delicate flight of a butterfly, these creatures are more wonderful than they may seem at first. Marvel at their complexity and reflect on how God values even the smallest aspects of life.

Pray:
Dear God, thank you for the beauty and complexity of all living things – even the smallest creatures. Help me to see your hand at work in every part of creation, and may I be filled with wonder at your intricate design. Amen.

June 9th

When you learn how to love (a fruit of the Spirit), you can experience the wonder of God's perfect love flowing through you to others.

Pursue Wonder:

Look for opportunities to love those around you with your words and actions today. The love you express comes from God, who is pure love and the ultimate source of all love. When you learn how to love more, you can experience the wonder of God's presence in a profound way, seeing God's heart for humanity mirrored in your words and actions.

Pray:

Dear God, teach me to love more deeply. Help me to embrace your complete and unconditional love for me, and to share the wonder of your love through my relationships with other people. Amen.

June 10th

By cultivating joy (a fruit of the Spirit), you can experience the wonder of God's goodness in any circumstances.

Pursue Wonder:

Joy is not dependent on your circumstances but on the knowledge that God is with you and working all things for good. Today, seek joy in the simple moments of your life and remember that God is with you there. You may enjoy the warmth of the sun, the laughter of a friend, the taste of a delicious meal, or any other simple blessing. By choosing to notice and celebrate small blessings, you'll discover more about the wonder of God's goodness to you.

Pray:

Dear God, help me to cultivate a spirit of joy in all circumstances. Let me see your extraordinary goodness even in the ordinary moments of my life. May your joy overflow in my heart today. Amen.

June 11th

As you develop peace (a fruit of the Spirit) in your heart and mind, you can experience the wonder of resting in God's care with confidence.

Pursue Wonder:
Today, intentionally seek peace in the middle of your daily activities. Spend a few moments in prayer, asking God to calm your heart and mind. During times of stress or frustration today, pause and breathe, remembering that God offers peace that surpasses all understanding. As you receive this peace, you'll be able to notice God's gentle yet powerful work in your life in all situations.

Pray:
Dear God, fill my heart with your peace today. In moments of chaos or anxiety, help me to trust you and rest with confidence that you will take good care of me in every situation I face. Amen.

June 12th

You can experience God's wonder when you practice patience (a fruit of the Spirit), trusting God's perfect timing and learning to see glimpses of God's work even in the waiting.

Pursue Wonder:

Practice patience today in both small and large situations. Whether you're waiting in line or waiting for an answer to prayer, remind yourself that God is at work with perfect timing. Patience allows you to step back and see how God weaves good purposes into your life. Instead of rushing through the day, slow down and savor the moments, trusting that God's timing is always best. In that trust, you'll discover wonder in God's unfolding plan.

Pray:

Dear God, teach me to be patient in every situation. Please help me trust in your timing and see glimpses of your work while I wait. May I experience the wonder of experiencing your perfect plan, even when I don't yet see the full picture of it. Amen.

June 13th

You can experience the wonder of God's love as you practice kindness (a fruit of the Spirit), sharing God's love in simple acts that bring positive change to others' lives and your own.

Pursue Wonder:

Today, look for ways to be kind to someone, such as through a smile, practical help with something, or words of encouragement. Simple, intentional acts of kindness reflect God's heart and can have positive ripple effects far beyond what you see. Notice how these small gestures create a sense of connection and gratitude that deepen your awareness of God's love. In these moments, you will experience the wonder of God's kindness flowing through you to bless others.

Pray:

Dear God, help me to reflect your love today through kind acts and words. Open my eyes to opportunities to bless others, and may I experience the wonder of your love at work through me. Amen.

June 14th

When you pursue goodness (a fruit of the Spirit), you can experience God's wonder by living with holiness in a world that longs for integrity and compassion.

Pursue Wonder:

Actively choose goodness today by seeking ways to make choices that align with God's holy character. Every act of goodness – such as honesty, generosity, or standing up for what's right – reflects the image of God in you. As you walk in goodness, you'll see the beauty of God's moral order and the impact it has on those around you. The wonder of God's goodness in your life reveals itself when you intentionally align your actions with God's will.

Pray:

Dear God, thank you for the gift of goodness. Help me to pursue it in all I do today, making decisions that reflect your heart. Let me see the wonder of living in alignment with your holiness. Amen.

June 15th

You can experience the wonder of God's faithfulness as you grow in faithfulness (a fruit of the Spirit), with the confidence that God is faithful and calls you to reflect that same commitment and dedication in your life.

Pursue Wonder:
Consider how you can show faithfulness today in your commitments – to family, friends, work, and more. When you are faithful in small things, you mirror God's unwavering loyalty and dependability. Faithfulness opens the door to deeper relationships and a stronger connection with God, as you see God's faithfulness to you even more clearly. Through consistent and devoted actions, you'll discover the wonder of God's enduring presence in your life.

Pray:
Dear God, thank you for your constant love and care. Please help me to be faithful in all I do today. May I see the wonder of your work in my life as I do my best to live with commitment and dedication. Amen.

June 16th

By practicing gentleness (a fruit of the Spirit), you can experience God's wonder by reflecting God's gentle compassion, bringing peace and healing to those around you.

Pursue Wonder:
Focus on being gentle in your interactions with people today. Gentleness is not weakness. Instead, it's strength under control. It's

an important way to reflect God's compassionate nature. As you handle situations with care and speak with grace, you'll notice the wonder of how gentleness softens hearts and builds trust. In moments of stress or conflict, respond with gentleness and see how that creates space for God's peace and healing to flow.

Pray:
Dear God, cultivate a spirit of gentleness in me today. Help me to reflect your compassionate nature when I interact with people. Let me witness the wonder of how your gentleness brings peace and healing when it flows through my life. Amen.

June 17th

You can experience the wonder of freedom through self-control (a fruit of the Spirit), as God empowers you to make the best choices.

Pursue Wonder:
Today, focus on practicing self-control in one area of your life where you would like to improve your habits – such as managing time, managing money, or managing the ways you eat or exercise. Self-control allows you to break free from impulsive behaviors and align your life with God's will. As you practice self-control, you'll discover the wonder of living with greater purpose, clarity, and peace.

Pray:
Dear God, please give me the strength to practice self-control today. Help me to make choices that honor you and lead to freedom

and joy. May I experience the wonder of living in alignment with your wisdom. Amen.

June 18th

Rivers and streams that flow with graceful power reflect the wonder of God's strength.

Pursue Wonder:
 Visit a river or stream and watch it flow with graceful power. Consider how God's strength flows through your life with power and grace.

Pray:
 Dear God, thank you for the wondrous strength of rivers and streams that reflect your graceful power. Help me to rely on your strength and to flow with your grace in my life. Amen.

June 19th

As you gather with others for summer celebrations, you can share the wonder of God's joy together.

Pursue Wonder:
 Participate in a summer celebration gathering. Enjoy your time there, and reflect on how God is there with you all, making the good time together possible.

Pray:

Dear God, thank you for the enjoyable summer celebrations that bring people together. Fill my heart with your joy and help me to share it with others. Amen.

June 20th

A summer picnic is a fun way to experience God's wonder through the beauty of creation and the simple blessing of food shared outdoors.

Pursue Wonder:

Today, plan a picnic lunch in your backyard, at a local park, or in any outdoor space that allows you to soak in the warmth of the season. As you enjoy the food and fresh air, take a moment to thank God for your food and the beauty of his creation around you. A picnic gives you an opportunity to connect with God through nature and celebrate his wonderful provision for you in all areas of your life.

Pray:

Dear God, thank you for the beauty of summer and for the blessing of food that nourishes me. As I enjoy this meal outdoors, help me to notice and celebrate the simple moments of wonder that you provide. Amen.

June 21st

You can see the wonder of God's work as the longest day of the year fills the world with light.

Pursue Wonder:

Enjoy the longest day of the year by spending time outside today. Reflect on how God's beauty fills the world with light.

Pray:

Dear God – Light of the World – thank you for the beauty of the longest day of the year. Please fill my life with your light and help me to shine your love into the world. Amen.

June 22nd

The balance of day and night reflects the wonder of God's wisdom and teaches you the importance of harmonious balance.

Pursue Wonder:

Enjoy watching a sunset this evening and reflect on the balance of day and night while you watch. Consider how God's wisdom teaches you harmony and balance in your life.

Pray:

Dear God, thank you for the balance of day and night that reflects your wonderful wisdom. Help me to seek harmony and balance in my life and to trust in your wise guidance. Amen.

June 23rd

God's wondrous grace and mercy are like raindrops that wash over you and renew you.

Pursue Wonder:

If it rains today where you live, take a walk in the rain and consider how God showers you with his renewing grace and mercy every day. If it's not raining where you live, watch a brief video of rain, and let it inspire you to remember that God showers you with grace and mercy daily.

Pray:

Dear God, thank you for rain showers that remind me of your grace and mercy. Please wash over me with your renewing grace and mercy today and every day of my life. Amen.

June 24th

The variety of life at the beach showcases God's wonderful creativity.

Pursue Wonder:

Visit a beach on this summer day and notice the variety of life there – from seagulls to starfish. Reflect on how each creature's unique design shows the wonder of God's creativity.

Pray:

Dear God, thank you for the variety of beach life that showcases your creativity. Help me to appreciate the uniqueness of each creature and to marvel at your wonderful creativity in my life, as well. Amen.

June 25th

You can experience the wonder of God's loving care through the warmth that envelops you on a summer evening.

Pursue Wonder:
   Spend time outside during a warm summer evening. Consider how the warmth of God's love envelops you with his care.

Pray:
   Dear God, thank you for the warmth of a summer evening that reminds me of your warm loving care. Help me to feel your love and to be comforted by your presence. Amen.

June 26th

The wondrous night sky reveals God's vastness and majesty, reminding you that the Creator of the universe is also personally involved in your life.

Pursue Wonder:
   Step outside tonight and look up at the stars. As you gaze at the night sky, let the sheer vastness of the universe fill you with awe. Each star is a reminder of how small you are in comparison to God's

creation – yet God knows you intimately and cares deeply for you. Spend a few moments in prayer, praising God for the wonder of his majesty and his personal love for you.

Pray:
　Dear God, as I gaze at the stars, I'm in awe of how vast you are, and yet you care personally for me. Thank you for knowing me personally and for caring for every detail of my life, even as you rule over the vastness of the universe. Amen.

June 27th

You can see the wonder of God's provision in the abundance of summer fruit.

Pursue Wonder:
　Enjoy some fresh summer fruit in different varieties today – berries, melons, citrus fruit, and more. Reflect on how God's provision offers nourishment and delight in your life.

Pray:
　Dear God, thank you for the abundance of summer fruit you've designed. Help me to appreciate your provision today and every day. Amen.

June 28th

Towering mountains reflect God's wondrous strength.

Pursue Wonder:

If possible, visit a mountain today. If not, look at pictures of mountains. Reflect on how tall mountains reflect God's towering strength in your life.

Pray:

Dear God, thank you for the towering mountains that reflect your strength. Help me to rely on your unlimited strength and to stand firm in my faith through all the challenges I face. Amen.

June 29th

You can experience the wonder of God's joy by embracing moments of playful fun, which refreshes your soul and reminds you of God's delight in your well-being.

Pursue Wonder:

Today, make space for play – through a game with your children or with friends, through a fun outdoor activity, or something else playful that brings you joy. Play is a form of worship when you engage with the lightness of life that God provides. Take time to relax and laugh, remembering that God invites you to enjoy his creation and the gift of life itself. In the joy of play, you'll discover the wonder of how God uses simple moments to restore and refresh your spirit.

Pray:

God, thank you for the gift of play. Help me to embrace moments of fun with gratitude. May I experience the wonder of life's lighter moments as part of your plan for my refreshment and joy. Amen.

June 30th

You can see the wonder of God's artistry in a summer sunset.

Pursue Wonder:
Watch the sunset and marvel at its beauty. Reflect on how God's wondrous artistry is evident in the colors of the sky.

Pray:
Dear God, thank you for the stunning sunsets of summer that showcase your artistry. Help me to appreciate the beauty of your creative design for this planet in every sunset I see. Amen.

JULY

July 1st

Every day is a new opportunity to encounter God's grace. You can embrace the wonder of fresh starts and new beginnings as an invitation to step into God's ongoing work in your life.

Pursue Wonder:
As you begin a new month, reflect on the areas where God is calling you to start fresh. This is a time to move forward with hope into something new, such as a new habit, a renewed mindset, or a commitment to deepen your faith. Write down one way you'd like to grow this month and invite God to work in that area. In each small beginning, you'll discover the wonder of God's constant renewal and grace.

Pray:
Dear God, thank you for the gift of fresh starts. Help me to embrace this new month with hope and trust in your work in my life. May I experience the wonder of your grace in each new day. Amen.

July 2nd

You can experience the wonder of God's creativity when you step out of your routine to explore new places, near and far.

Pursue Wonder:
Take a walk or drive somewhere new today – such as a park, a museum, or a nearby town you've never visited before. Pay attention

to the details of your surroundings. Exploring unfamiliar places can open your eyes to God's creativity in ways you might not notice in your regular routine. As you immerse yourself in new sights, sounds, and experiences, let them remind you of the vastness of God's creation and the beauty God has placed in the world for you to enjoy.

Pray:
　Dear God, open my eyes to see the wonder of new places today. Help me to explore with gratitude for your creativity and love. May each new experience draw me closer to you. Amen.

July 3rd

Summer vacations offer a chance to step away from your routine and see God's wonder in new places and experiences. You can find God's presence in the adventure and rest that vacations provide.

Pursue Wonder:
　Enjoy a vacation this summer, and wherever you go, be intentional about experiencing God's wonder there. As you enjoy a change of scenery – in a different nation, a different state, or a place you'd like to visit that's close to home – look for what inspires you and gives you glimpses of God at work. Include some time for both adventurous discovery and peaceful rest; both types of vacation experiences can draw you closer to God.

Pray:
　Dear God, thank you for the gift of rest and for the beauty of your creation that I can enjoy during this season. Help me to experience

your wonder in new places and to return from this time inspired and refreshed by your presence. Amen.

July 4th

You can celebrate the God-given wonder of freedom as you enjoy the blessings of liberty.

Pursue Wonder:
    Reflect on the freedoms you enjoy. Consider how these freedoms are gifts from God, and thank God for the ability to live in liberty.

Pray:
    Dear God, thank you for the blessings of liberty. Help me to use my freedoms wisely and to honor you in all I do. Amen.

July 5th

You can find God's wonderful peace in the calm after storms.

Pursue Wonder:
    After a summer storm, take some time to appreciate the calm that follows. Reflect on how God's peace reassures you in the storms of life.

Pray:

Dear God, thank you for the calm that follows the storms in my life. Help me to rest in your constant presence and to find peace in your care. Amen.

July 6th

The wonder of God's love comes through kindness – even the kindness of strangers.

Pursue Wonder:
Notice acts of kindness from strangers today, and appreciate how these moments reflect God's love and care for all people.

Pray:
Dear God, thank you for the kindness of strangers that reflects your love. Help me to spread your love through kindness to everyone I meet. Amen.

July 7th

God's wondrous strength is like a towering tree that is deeply rooted and unshakable.

Pursue Wonder:
Look at a tall tree, such as an oak or a sycamore, and consider its deep roots and strength. Consider how God's strength supports and sustains you.

Pray:

Dear God, thank you for the strength that sustains me through life's challenges. Help me to be deeply rooted in you, standing strong in my faith. Amen.

July 8th

You can experience the wonder of God's provision through water – a gift from God that nourishes, refreshes, and sustains life.

Pursue Wonder:

Today, when you interact with water (drinking, bathing, swimming, etc.), take the time to appreciate the wonder of this life-sustaining gift from God. Water is a symbol of renewal and refreshment, both physically and spiritually. Let water remind you of God's provision for your life, and God's offer of living water through Jesus to quench your soul's deepest thirst.

Pray:

Dear God, thank you for the gift of water that sustains and refreshes me. Help me to experience your wonder today as I use water, and may that remind me of your constant provision and love. Amen.

July 9th

You can encounter God's wonder in the quiet moments of your day, where God's peaceful voice speaks to your heart.

Pursue Wonder:

Today, find time to embrace silence – either just for a few minutes or longer, if possible. In a world full of noise, silence allows you to reconnect with God, listen for God's voice, and find peace in God's presence. As you intentionally create space for silence, notice how God speaks to you – not through the chaos, but through the stillness. You can experience the deep peace that only God can give.

Pray:

Dear God, help me to embrace silence today so I can hear your voice more clearly. In the quiet, may I experience the wonder of your presence and find peace in your love. Amen.

July 10th

You can see God's wonderful provision in the summer harvest that reminds you of God's faithful care.

Pursue Wonder:

Visit a farmers' market or enjoy fresh produce today. Consider how God provides for your needs and thank him for faithfully caring for you.

Pray:

Dear God, thank you for the summer harvest that reminds me of your care. Please help me to trust in your provision and to be grateful for your blessings. Amen.

July 11th

The stillness of a summer night that quiets your mind and heart can help you connect with God's wonderful peace.

Pursue Wonder:
Spend time outside on a quiet summer night, perhaps stargazing or listening to night sounds like crickets chirping. Reflect on how God's peace quiets your mind and heart.

Pray:
Dear God, thank you for the stillness of a summer night that quiets my mind and heart. Please fill me with your peace and help me to rest in your presence. Amen.

July 12th

Rest is a gift from God that renews your body, mind, and spirit. You can find wonder in the way God designed rest to refresh and restore you.

Pursue Wonder:
Make rest a priority today – through a nap, reading, or simply relaxing outside. Rest is important for your well-being. When you pause from the busyness, you allow yourself to recharge and reconnect with God. As you rest, reflect on how God is constantly at work, even when you're still. Rest helps reveals the wonder of God's constant care for you.

Pray:
Dear God, thank you for the gift of rest. Help me to pause today and experience the wonder of your care and renewal in my life. I trust you with all my worries and burdens as I rest in your presence. Amen.

July 13th

You can experience God's grace in a cool, refreshing summer breeze on a hot summer day.

Pursue Wonder:
Feel the cool breeze on this hot day and let it remind you of how God's grace refreshes your soul.

Pray:
Dear God, thank you for the refreshing breeze that reminds me of your grace. Let me be renewed by your love and share that grace with others. Amen.

July 14th

God's love is abundant, like the lush greenery of summer.

Pursue Wonder:
Walk through a park or garden and take in the lush greenery of

summer. Reflect on how God's love surrounds you with care and protection.

Pray:
Dear God, thank you for the wonderful abundance of your love that surrounds me like the greenery of summer. Please help me to feel your love and to share it with others. Amen.

July 15th

You can experience God's wonder as you trust God through life transitions and embrace the growth God brings you in each season.

Pursue Wonder:
Life is full of seasons that each bring its own challenges and joys. Take time today to reflect on the current season of your life. Are you in a season of growth, rest, challenge, or joy? No matter what, remember that God is with you in every moment. Ask God to reveal what he's teaching you in this season, and trust that God is personally guiding you through it with purpose.

Pray:
Dear God, thank you for the different seasons of life. Help me to trust you in this current season and to see the wonder of your presence and purpose in every stage. Amen.

July 16th

You can find God's joy in the simple pleasures of summer.

Pursue Wonder:

Enjoy a simple summer pleasure today, like ice cream, a walk in a park, or a picnic. Consider how these moments bring joy to your life.

Pray:

Dear God, thank you for the simple pleasures that bring joy to my days. Help me to find joy every day and to share that joy with others. Amen.

July 17th

God's wisdom is like the steady sun, offering light and clarity to your path.

Pursue Wonder:

Spend time in the sunlight today, reflecting on how God's wisdom brings enlightenment into your life. Consider how God's guidance leads you on the right path.

Pray:

Dear God, Light of the World, thank you for the light of your wisdom that guides my path. Help me to walk in your light and to trust in your guidance every day. Amen.

July 18th

You can experience God's peace through the calming rhythm of ocean waves.

Pursue Wonder:

If possible, visit the ocean and watch and listen to the rhythm of the waves. Reflect on how the calming movement and sound of the waves inspires you to think of God's peace and to pursue that peace by giving God your worries in prayer.

Pray:

Dear God, thank you for the calming rhythm of the ocean waves that reminds me of your peace. As I give my worries to you, I trust you to help me with each of those situations. Please help me to find peace in your presence and to carry that peace with me throughout the day. Amen.

JULY 19TH

Conversations can be filled with wonder when you listen for God's wisdom through them.

Pursue Wonder:

Today, be intentional about listening during your conversations. As you talk with family, friends, and even strangers, approach each conversation with curiosity and openness to what God might be saying through them. You can discover wonder by hearing someone's story, gaining a new perspective, or being reminded of God's wisdom. Let your own words reflect kindness and truth, and see how God uses your conversations today to inspire you with awe.

Pray:

Dear God, thank you for the gift of conversations with the people in my life. Help me to listen well today, speak with grace, and be open to finding your wonder in each conversation. Please align my heart and mind your love. Amen.

July 20th

Your Creator God has made you in his image, so you can experience God's wonder through your own acts of creativity.

Pursue Wonder:

Take time today to enjoy a creative activity that inspires you. Let this be a time to reflect God's creative nature within you in some way – solving a problem, cooking, building, gardening, singing, writing, drawing, or working on another kind of project. As you express yourself, notice the wonder that comes from the creative process. Whenever you do something creative, you can encounter God at work, inspiring you.

Pray:

Dear God, thank you for the gift of creativity. As I create today, please let me experience the wonder of reflecting your image and find joy in the process of bringing something inspiring into the world. Amen.

July 21st

The night sky declares the glory of God. You can find wonder in the vastness of space, knowing that the same God who created the stars also knows and loves you personally.

Pursue Wonder:

Tonight, gaze up at the night sky. Let yourself be amazed by the sheer magnitude of God's creation – the stars, the moon, or just the deep dark expanse of the sky. As you look up, reflect on the wonder of God's power and presence. God not only placed every star in its place, but he also knows your heart intimately. The night sky can remind you of God's greatness and his care for you.

Pray:

Dear God, thank you for the beauty of the night sky and how it reminds me of your glory. Help me to see your wonder in the sky tonight and to remember how deeply you love me. Amen.

JULY 22ND

You can experience God's wonder when you serve others, reflecting God's love and care for the world through your actions.

Pursue Wonder:

Today, offer your time and kindness to someone you know who you can help somehow – such as through listening, words of encouragement, or a practical task like a chore or errand. As you serve, notice how God's love flows through you and into that person's life. Serving others not only blesses them, but it also opens your heart to the wonder of how God can work through you to bring more love into the world.

Pray:
Dear God, thank you for the opportunity to serve others. Help me to see the wonder of your love at work as I serve today. May I reflect your heart in my actions and bring your love to those around me. Amen.

July 23rd

As you endure summer's heat, God can teach you resilience and the importance of relying on his wondrous strength.

Pursue Wonder:
Endure the heat of a summer day and consider how it teaches you resilience. Reflect on how God's strength helps you endure challenges in every part of your life.

Pray:
Dear God, thank you for the strength that helps me endure the heat of challenges. Please help me to be resilient in my faith and to rely on your strength to empower me every day. Amen.

July 24th

The playful spirit of summer invites you to enjoy the wonderful blessings God pours into your life.

Pursue Wonder:
 Enjoy a playful summer activity today – such as an outdoor game or swimming – and celebrate the fun and joy that brings you.

Pray:
 Dear God, thank you for the playful spirit of summer that invites me to enjoy the blessings you're constantly giving me. Help me to embrace the wonder of play whenever I need encouragement. Amen.

July 25th

You can find the wonder of God's wisdom and peace in the natural balance of work and rest.

Pursue Wonder:
 Take time to rest today, honoring the balance of work and rest that God has established. Celebrate how this balance brings wisdom and peace to your life.

Pray:
 Dear God, thank you for the natural balance of work and rest you designed for well-being. Help me to balance the time I spend working and resting well. Amen.

July 26th

The still waters of a summer lake or pond can calm your heart and mind, reminding you of God's peace.

Pursue Wonder:

If possible, visit a lake or a pond today. Reflect on how the calmness of the water brings wonderful peace to your heart and mind.

Pray:

Dear God, thank you for the still waters that help me be calm and receive your peace. Let me find peace in your presence and carry that peace with me throughout the day. Amen.

July 27th

You can find God's wonder when you slow down and pay attention to God's extraordinary presence in ordinary moments.

Pursue Wonder:

Today, focus on appreciating the simple joys of life, such a hug, a song, or the laughter of a child. Sometimes, you can find wonder not in dramatic events but in the quiet, everyday experiences that inspire you. As you go about your day, look for the beauty in simple moments and let them remind you of God's constant presence in every detail of your life.

Pray:

Dear God, please help me to see the wonder in the simple moments today. Teach me to slow down, appreciate your presence, and enjoy the small yet significant blessings you have given me. Amen.

July 28th

Music has the power to stir your soul and connect you with God in wonderful ways.

Pursue Wonder:

Today, listen to music that inspires you. Let the music you choose draw you into a sense of awe for God's creativity and his ability to communicate to your soul through sound. You can also create your own music by singing or playing an instrument, offering it as an expression of praise to God.

Pray:

Dear God, thank you for the gift of music and the way it moves my soul. Help me to experience your wonder through the sounds I hear today, and let my heart be lifted in praise to you. Amen.

July 29th

The changing skies of summer showcase God's creativity.

Pursue Wonder:

Watch the sky throughout the day, noticing how it changes with the light, clouds, and colors. Enjoy the wonder of how the sky displays the Creator's creativity.

Pray:

Dear God, thank you for the constantly changing skies that showcase your creativity anytime and anywhere. Amen.

July 30th

God's grace is like the cool shade of a tree, offering you rest and refuge.

Pursue Wonder:

Sit under the shade of a tree today and feel the coolness it provides. Consider how God's grace offers you rest and refuge from the heat of life's challenges.

Pray:

Dear God, thank you for the cool shade on this hot summer day. Help me to find rest in your grace and to trust in your care through all seasons. Amen.

July 31st

Time is a gift from God, and you can experience God's wonder by being intentional about how you spend it, using each moment wisely.

Pursue Wonder:

As you close out this month, reflect on how you've used the time God has given you. Consider how you can be more intentional in the weeks ahead to prioritize time for activities that are important from God's perspective, such as prayer, meditation, relationships, and service. When you view time as a gift, you begin to see each day as an opportunity to experience God's wonder and make the most of every moment.

Pray:

Dear God, thank you for the gift of time. Help me to use my time wisely and intentionally, making space in my schedule for the things that matter most. May I experience your wonder in each moment of my day. Amen.

AUGUST

August 1st

The abundance of summer reminds you that God provides more than you need.

Pursue Wonder:
Notice the fullness of summer – such as the rich greenery, the abundance of fruit, and the long days. Reflect on how God provides abundantly in your life.

Pray:
Dear God, thank you for the abundance of summer that reminds me of your generous provision. Please help me to trust in your generosity and to share your blessings with others. Amen.

August 2nd

Early mornings invite you to start each day with God in peaceful stillness that helps you notice God's wonderful presence.

Pursue Wonder:
Wake up early and spend a few moments in the stillness of the morning. Enjoy how you encounter the wonder of God's presence with you there.

Pray:
Dear God, thank you for the stillness of early mornings that

invite me to start my day with you. Help me to carry your wondrous peace with me throughout the day. Amen.

August 3rd

Summer fruit and vegetables show the wonder of God's creativity.

Pursue Wonder:
    Visit a local farmers' market and buy a variety of produce. At home, take time to savor each flavor of various fruit and vegetables and appreciate how God designed them for your health and enjoyment. Reflect on how even simple sensory experiences – like the taste of a peach or the color of corn – are gifts from God.

Pray:
    Dear God, thank you for the summer fruit and vegetables that show me your creativity in different ways. Help me to appreciate the uniqueness of each creation. Amen.

August 4th

Friendship is a gift from God, and you can find wonder in the love and connection you share with friends.

Pursue Wonder:
    Today, reach out to a friend and spend quality time together, in person, on the phone, or online. Reflect on how God uses friendship

to strengthen and encourage you. As you enjoy each other's company, let the wonder of God's love for you both deepen your appreciation for the relationships God has placed in your life.

Pray:
 Dear God, thank you for the gift of friendship. Help me to treasure the connections you've blessed me with and to pursue your wonder together with my friends. Amen.

August 5th

Family is a reflection of God's love, and you can experience God's wonder in the relationships God has given you within your family.

Pursue Wonder:
 Spend time with your family today, enjoying something meaningful like a shared meal, a conversation, or an outing. Reflect on the ways God has blessed you through these relationships – even in stressful situations. Look for moments of connection and love, and let those remind you of God's wonderful presence with you all.

Pray:
 Dear God, thank you for the gift of my family. Help me to see your wonder in the love that we share, no matter what disagreements we may have with each other. Amen.

August 6th

You can honor God and experience God's wonder through physical exercise.

Pursue Wonder:
Today, enjoy physical exercise, such as walking, swimming, dancing, or a gym workout. As you move, reflect on the wonderful design of your body and the gift of health. Let your exercise be an act of gratitude for the body God has given you and a way to experience the wonder of God's creation through yourself.

Pray:
Dear God, thank you for the gift of my body and the ability to move. Help me to care for it well and to experience your wonder through each step I take today. Amen.

August 7th

Strong summer storms can remind you of God's wondrous strength.

Pursue Wonder:
If a summer storm occurs today, watch the power of the wind and rain. If you can't watch a storm in person, watch a video of a summer storm online. Consider how God's strength is both powerful and protective in your life.

Pray:
Dear God, thank you for the strength and protection you give me

in the storms of life. Help me to trust in your power and to find safety in your care. Amen.

August 8th

God's grace is as refreshing as a cool drink on a hot day.

Pursue Wonder:
Enjoy a cool drink today and let it remind you of God's refreshing grace, which quenches the thirst of your soul.

Pray:
Dear God, thank you for the wonder of your refreshing grace. Help me to drink deeply of your love and to share that grace with others. Amen.

August 9th

Serving others is a powerful way to experience God's love flowing through you and discover wonder in the process.

Pursue Wonder:
Find an opportunity today to serve your community – such as helping a neighbor or working on a local volunteer project. As you give your time and effort, open your heart to the joy of serving others. Notice how God's love flows through you to those in need, and reflect on the blessing of being a part of God's work in the world.

Pray:

Dear God, thank you for the privilege of serving others. Help me to find wonder in each act of service and to be a reflection of your love to those around me. Amen.

August 10th

Through the process of cooking a meal, you can find wonder in the creativity and nourishment that God offers.

Pursue Wonder:

Today, cook a meal mindfully. As you chop, stir, and season, consider how God provides for your physical needs and how cooking can be an expression of care for yourself and others. Savor the process, and take time to enjoy the food as a reminder of God's wondrous provision.

Pray:

Dear God, thank you for the gift of food and the ability to create nourishing meals. Help me to see your wonder in the process of cooking and to be grateful for your constant provision. Amen.

August 11th

You can experience God's wonder when you face a problem and rely on God's guidance to find a solution.

Pursue Wonder:

Today, approach any problems you face with an attitude of trust in God's guidance. As you work through solutions, ask God for wisdom and direction. Notice how God leads you toward the best decisions, and enjoy the wonder of seeing solutions come to life in each situation.

Pray:

Dear God, thank you for the wisdom you provide. Help me to rely on your guidance in every challenge I face today, and let me see the wonder of you helping me solve problems. Amen.

August 12th

God's joy is contagious, spreading through the smiles and laughter of those around you.

Pursue Wonder:

Share a smile or laughter with someone today. Reflect on how God's joy spreads through your relationships.

Pray:

Dear God, thank you for the smiles and laughter that spread your joy. Help me to share your joy through all of my relationships. Amen.

August 13th

God's wisdom is like the steady growth of a tree that points to the importance of patience and perseverance.

Pursue Wonder:
Visit a mature tree that has stood for many years. Reflect on how its steady growth is a lesson in patience and perseverance, guided by the wisdom of God's design.

Pray:
Dear God, thank you for the steady growth that teaches me the importance of patience and perseverance. Help me to trust in your timing and to grow steadily in faith. Amen.

August 14th

God's love is boundless, like the vast expanse of the summer sky.

Pursue Wonder:
Look up at the sky today and take in its vastness. Reflect on how God's love is boundless and reaches every corner of your life.

Pray:
Dear God, thank you for the boundless love that fills my life like the vast summer sky. Help me to feel your love in every moment and to share it freely with others. Amen.

August 15th

God's strength is like the resilience of the summer sun that shines brightly even after storms.

Pursue Wonder:
Notice how the sun shines brightly after a summer storm. Consider how God's strength helps you to shine, even after facing life's storms.

Pray:
Dear God, thank you for the resilience that allows me to shine after life's storms. Help me to rely on your strength and to be a light to others. Amen.

August 16th

Silence offers you a sacred space to encounter God's presence and reflect on God's wonder.

Take a break today from the noise and distractions of life. Find a quiet place to sit in silence, breathe deeply, and focus on God's presence with you. In the silence, allow yourself to rest in the peace that comes from being fully present with God. Silence can reveal God's wonder in ways that you can miss in noisy environments.

Pray:
Dear God, thank you for the gift of silence. Help me to find your presence in the stillness today and to listen for your voice as I reflect on your wonder. Amen.

August 17th

You can see the wonder of God's provision and timing in the cycles of nature, as God provides for every creature in its time.

Pursue Wonder:
Pay attention to the cycles of nature around you – animals gathering food, plants blooming or bearing fruit, etc. Reflect on how God provides for every part of his creation in its time.

Pray:
Dear God, thank you for the cycles of nature that reflect your provision. Help me to trust that you will provide for all of my needs in your perfect timing. Amen.

August 18th

The world is filled with details that reflect God's intricate creativity. You can experience God's wonder when you take the time to observe the small details around you.

Pursue Wonder:
Today, slow down and intentionally observe the details around you – like the pattern of leaves on a tree, the colors of a sunset, or the melody in a song you enjoy. Open your senses to the intricate creativity in the world, and let those small details draw you closer to God, the ultimate Creator.

Pray:

Dear God, thank you for the beauty that surrounds me. Help me to slow down today and open my eyes to the wonder of the details in your creation. Amen.

August 19th

You can see the wonder of God's wisdom in the harmony of nature, where each element works together in balance.

Pursue Wonder:

Take a walk in nature and notice how different elements – trees, water, animals, etc. – work together in harmony. Reflect on how God's wisdom brings balance to the world.

Pray:

Dear God, thank you for the harmony of nature that reflects your wisdom. Help me to find balance in my life and to trust in your guiding hand. Amen.

August 20th

God's love is like a sheltering tree, offering protection and comfort in all seasons.

Pursue Wonder:

Find a tree that provides shade and shelter, and spend some time under its branches. Reflect on how God's love offers you protection and comfort in every season.

Pray:
　　Dear God, thank you for the protection and comfort that your love provides. Help me to rest in your care with peace. Amen.

August 21st

Each step you take on a hiking trail is a step toward discovering God's wonder in creation and your own life.

Pursue Wonder:
　　Today, take a hike on a trail outdoors. As you walk, pay attention to the changing terrain, the plants, and the wildlife you see. Reflect on how the journey mirrors your walk with God, filled with challenges, beauty, and growth. Let the adventure of exploring nature remind you of the adventure of faith.

Pray:
　　Dear God, as I walk through your creation today, help me to see your wonder in every step I take. Guide me on the path you have set for me, and help me to embrace the adventure of following you. Amen.

August 22nd

Visiting a museum allows you to explore the wonder of human ingenuity and the divine inspiration behind it.

Pursue Wonder:

Plan a visit to a museum today and enjoy learning about the museum's focus – on history, science, art, or something else. As you explore the exhibits, reflect on how God has given humanity the creativity and curiosity to make discoveries. Each artifact or artwork can serve as a reminder of God's wonder, from the grand ideas to the smallest details.

Pray:

Dear God, thank you for the creativity and knowledge you've given to humanity. As I explore today, help me to see your wonder in the works of history, science, and art. Please inspire me to learn and create in ways that honor you. Amen.

August 23rd

Playing or watching a sports event can inspire you to appreciate the wonder of how God gives people strength.

Pursue Wonder:

Watch a sports game or play a sport you enjoy today. Pay attention to the mental strength of strategy and teamwork and the physical strength of the athletes. Feel the thrill of the game and consider how the competition and camaraderie inspire you to appreciate how God empowers people to be strong.

Pray:

Dear God, thank you for the joy of sports and the opportunity to see the wonder of how you give people strength. Help me to celebrate the gifts you've given me through healthy competition and the joy of community. Amen.

August 24th

The gentle rhythm of paddling through water can help you experience the wonder of God's peace in your life.

Pursue Wonder:

Today, try kayaking or canoeing in a river or lake. As you paddle through the water, reflect on the calm and strength you find in God's presence. The peaceful flow of water can remind you of God's steady guidance and care for you. Let the adventure of exploring the water help you focus on the beauty and peace God offers.

Pray:

Dear God, thank you for the peace and beauty of the water around me. As I paddle today, help me to feel your presence, guiding me through both still and rushing waters. Let this adventure bring me closer to you. Amen.

August 25th

You can see God's wisdom in the rhythms of life that teach you to live in sync with God's timing.

Pursue Wonder:

Consider the daily, weekly, and seasonal rhythms in your life. Reflect on how living in sync with God's timing brings you wisdom and peace.

Pray:

Dear God, thank you for the rhythms of life that teach me to live in sync with your timing. Help me to follow your lead and to find peace in your perfect timing. Amen.

August 26th

God's love is like a summer breeze, gently reminding you of God's constant presence.

Pursue Wonder:

Feel the summer breeze on your face and let it remind you of God's constant loving presence with you. Thank God for how he is always with you, gently encouraging you whenever you reach out to him.

Pray:

Dear God, thank you for the gentle breeze that reminds me of your constant presence. Help me to feel your love throughout my day today. Amen.

August 27th

Sturdy trees that stand tall through every storm reflect the wonder of God's strength.

Pursue Wonder:
Stand beside a tall, sturdy tree and feel its strength. Reflect on how God's strength helps you stand tall through the storms of life.

Pray:
Dear God, thank you for the strength that helps me stand tall through life's storms. Help me to remain rooted in faith and to trust in your power each day. Amen.

August 28th

You can experience the wonder of God's peace in the evening transition from day to night.

Pursue Wonder:
This evening, watch the daylight fade into the darkness of night, with a colorful sunset along the way. Reflect on how God's wondrous peace calms your heart and prepares you for rest.

Pray:
Dear God, thank you for the evening light that calms my heart and mind as the day ends. Help me to rest in your peace and to trust in your care through the night. Amen.

August 29th

Your wonderful God provides all the food you need every day and encourages you to trust in his care day by day.

Pursue Wonder:
   Before you eat your meals today, say grace to thank God for providing for your needs today and every day.

Pray:
   Dear God, thank you for the daily bread that reminds me of your care. Help me to trust in your daily provision and to be content with what you provide. Amen.

August 30th

By playing games in the fresh air, you can experience God's wonderful gift of play.

Pursue Wonder:
   Today, organize or join an outdoor game with friends or family – such as frisbee, volleyball, or another favorite game. As you play, feel the energy in your body, the fresh air on your skin, and the connection with others. Let this fun time together bring you into a deeper appreciation of God's gift of play.

Pray:

Dear God, thank you for the gift of fun and for the simple joy of playing games outside. Help me to see your wonder in every moment we play, and to appreciate the gift of fun time with people I love. Amen.

August 31st

On a road trip, you can discover the wonder of God's creation and God's guidance for your life.

Pursue Wonder:

A road trip gives you a chance to see new places, encounter different people, and experience the freedom of the open road. Plan a road trip today – either a short drive or a longer adventure. As you travel, take in the changing scenery and reflect on how God leads you through different seasons and places in life. Every stop along the way is an opportunity to encounter something new about God's creation or God's guidance for you. Embrace the spontaneity of the journey and trust that God is with you as you travel every mile of it.

Pray:

Dear God, thank you for the adventure of travel. As I drive on the road today, help me to see your wonder in every place I visit and in each new experience. I choose to trust in your guidance through life's many roads. Amen.

SEPTEMBER

September 1st

As summer begins to wane, God reminds you that each season has its own wonderful beauty and purpose.

Pursue Wonder:
Notice the subtle changes in nature as summer transitions to fall. Reflect on how God has a purpose for every season in your life.

Pray:
Dear God, thank you for the beauty and purpose I can discover in every phase of life. Help me to embrace each season and to find you guiding me through them. Amen.

September 2nd

When you read, you're participating in the wonder of learning that God designed for you.

Pursue Wonder:
Books open doors to wonderful new worlds, perspectives, and understanding. Today, dive into a book on a subject that fascinates you. As you read, remember that God gave you the capacity to learn and grow, filling your mind with insights that reflect his wisdom. Allow the act of learning through reading to remind you of the vastness of God's knowledge and the joy God gives you when you discover something new.

Pray:

Dear God, thank you for the gift of books and for the chance to grow in knowledge. Help me to turn that knowledge into wisdom by applying it to my life in the best ways. Amen.

September 3rd

Pursuing new skills brings you closer to understanding God's boundless creativity.

Pursue Wonder:

Challenge yourself today to learn a new skill, such as learning how to cook a new dish, play a musical instrument, or speak a different language. Engage in the process with patience and curiosity. As you practice and improve, celebrate how each step in learning is a reflection of God's wonderful faithfulness in guiding you.

Pray:

Dear God, help me to approach the challenge of learning something new with joy and determination. Thank you for the chance to develop skills that reflect your creativity and ingenuity. Amen.

September 4th

As the days grow shorter, God teaches you the value of rest and reflection.

Pursue Wonder:
Notice how the days are beginning to shorten. Use this time to rest and reflect on the wonder of God's work in your life.

Pray:
Dear God, thank you for the shortening days that remind me to slow down and reflect. Help me to find rest in you and to use this time for renewal. Amen.

September 5th

God's provision in the harvest season reminds you of the wonderful reality that God meets your needs in every season of life.

Pursue Wonder:
Think about the harvests taking place this month. Reflect on how God has provided for you in this season and throughout your life.

Pray:
Dear God, thank you for always providing what I need. Help me to trust in your care during every season of my life. Amen.

September 6th

Learning from your mistakes can lead to some of the most profound moments of wonder in your walk with God.

Pursue Wonder:

Take time today to reflect on a recent mistake you made. Rather than dwelling on it with regret, consider what God might be teaching you through the experience. Ask for wisdom to grow from it and look for the wonder in how God uses even your mistakes for good purposes. Trust that God's grace will transform every failure into a learning opportunity.

Pray:

Dear God, thank you for turning my mistakes into learning experiences. Please give me the humility to grow and the faith to trust your grace in every moment. Amen.

September 7th

God's love is wondrous like the golden light of September – warm and enduring as the seasons change.

Pursue Wonder:

Notice the warm, golden light of the early autumn sun. Thank God for how his love for you remains constant and enduring, even as the seasons change.

Pray:

Dear God, thank you for the golden light of September that reminds me of your enduring love. Help me to feel your warmth and to trust in your constant care. Amen.

September 8th

The wisdom and encouragement you receive from others can reveal God's wonder as you learn from them.

Pursue Wonder:
God designed you to learn and grow in community. Today, seek out a conversation with someone whose perspective or expertise is different from yours. Learn from a friend, family member, or mentor. The wonder of learning through others reveals the wonder of diverse gifts from God.

Pray:
Dear God thank you for the gift of community. Help me to learn from those around me and to share my own knowledge generously. May I keep growing in love and understanding. Amen.

September 9th

Reflection offers space to learn from past experiences and to recognize God's wonder in every season.

Pursue Wonder:
Today, set aside time for quiet reflection. Review the past few months and consider the lessons you've learned, the challenges you've overcome, and the blessings you've experienced. As you reflect, listen for God's voice, guiding you into a deeper under-

standing and appreciation for God's work in your life. Let this reflection inspire you with awe.

Pray:
Dear God, thank you for the gift of reflection. Help me to look back on my life with gratitude and to learn from each experience you've brought me through. May I see the wonder of your work in every season and trust your guidance for the future. Amen.

SEPTEMBER 10TH

God's ways are often mysterious, beyond your understanding. Yet, in those mysteries, you can discover great wonder.

Pursue Wonder:
Today, reflect on a situation in your life that feels uncertain or unclear. Rather than trying to solve every mystery, let yourself rest in the wonder of not knowing. Trust that God is working behind the scenes, weaving together good plans for you. As you lean into the mystery, allow it to deepen your awe for the God who knows everything.

Pray:
Dear God, please help me to embrace the mysteries of life with faith, knowing that your wisdom far surpasses mine. Teach me to find wonder in the unknown and trust that you are working all things for good. Amen.

September 11th

Serving others teaches you about God's wonderful love in action.

Pursue Wonder:
    Every act of service welcomes God's love to flow through your life into other people's lives. Find an opportunity today to serve someone in your community, such as helping a neighbor or volunteering at a local organization. As you serve, keep your heart open to learning. Through service, you can discover the wonder of God's love poured out in tangible ways, and you will experience God working through your efforts.

Pray:
    Dear God, please teach me the beauty of serving others and how I can grow in your love through service. Help me to see the wonder of you at work through me when I serve. Amen.

September 12th

When you release your anxieties to God, you open yourself to experience the wondrous peace that comes from trusting in God's care for you.

Pursue Wonder:
    Worry can cloud your vision of God's wonder. Take a few moments today to identify the worries that are distracting you. In prayer, hand them over to God, asking him to replace them with

peace. As you let go of your anxieties, notice how much more clearly you can see the wonder in your life. God's peace gives you the freedom to focus on his wonderful work around you.

Pray:
    Dear God, I surrender my worries to you. Please fill me with your peace so I can see and experience the wonder of your presence in every moment. Help me to trust in your provision and care. Thank you, God. Amen.

September 13th

When you fully trust God to guide your steps, you can approach life with confidence, knowing God is with you.

Pursue Wonder:
    Confidence isn't about relying on your own abilities; it's about trusting in God's strength and direction. Reflect on an area of your life where you feel uncertain or lacking in confidence. Instead of focusing on your limitations, pray for God's guidance. As you place your trust in God, walk boldly in the assurance that God will give you the wisdom and strength you need. Confidence in God's guidance opens the door to experiencing God's wonder in every situation.

Pray:
    Dear God, I trust you and ask for your guidance. Help me to walk with confidence, knowing that you're directing my path. Thank you for the wonder I experience when I rely on your strength and wisdom. Amen.

September 14th

When you boldly rely on God's promises, you can experience God's wonder in abundance.

Pursue Wonder:
God has given you promises that are unshakable. Take time today to reflect on the promises God has made to you in the Bible. As you meditate on God's Word, declare those promises over your life, replacing fear with faith. Boldly trusting God's promises will opens doors to experiencing abundant wonder in your life.

Pray:
Dear God, thank you for the promises in your Word. Help me to boldly stand on your truth and walk in the confidence that your plans for me are full of hope and wonder. Amen.

September 15th

You can see God's strength reflected in the endurance of nature, which is steadfast through every season.

Pursue Wonder:
Notice how God's creation remains steadfast through the changing seasons. Reflect on how God's strength helps you remain steady and unshaken through the ups and downs of life.

Pray:

Dear God, thank you for the strength that helps me remain steady through life's changes. Help me to trust in your power and to stand firm in faith. Amen.

September 16th

Stepping into the unknown can be frightening, but it is also where you encounter God's most profound wonders.

Pursue Wonder:

Consider an area of your life where you feel uncertain or unsure of the next step. Instead of holding back in fear, take a step forward in faith, trusting God to guide you. In the unknown, you will discover God's presence in a deeper way. That will help you experience the wonder of God leading you into new possibilities.

Pray:

Dear God, give me the courage to step into the unknown with faith, knowing that you are always with me. Help me to experience the wonder of your guidance and to trust you in every season. Amen.

September 17th

The Bible is God's living Word, full of wisdom and wonder for every area of life.

Pursue Wonder:

As you read and meditate on the Bible, you open yourself up to the lifelong learning that God desires for you. Today, spend extra time reading and studying the Bible. Choose a passage or book you haven't explored in a while. As you read, ask the Holy Spirit to reveal new insights that will deepen your understanding of God's character and his plans for you. Be open to the wonder of how God speaks to you through the Bible's living words.

Pray:

Dear God, thank you for your wonderful Word. Help me to approach the Bible as a lifelong learner, eager to discover the truths you have for me today. Amen.

SEPTEMBER 18TH

By choosing faith over doubt, you open yourself to the wonder of seeing God at work in the middle of uncertainty.

Pursue Wonder:

Doubt can creep in, making you question God's plans or presence. Today, whenever doubt arises, counter it with a declaration of faith. Speak God's promises aloud and remind yourself of God's past faithfulness. As you choose faith over doubt, watch how God reveals his wonder in unexpected ways. Faith brings you closer to God and opens your eyes to God's incredible work.

Pray:

Dear God, please strengthen my faith when doubt tries to take hold. Help me to trust your promises and to see your wonder in every situation, even when I don't understand what you're doing. Amen.

September 19th

God's love is like the first fall leaves – a wonderful sign of beauty in the middle of change.

Pursue Wonder:
Notice the first fall leaves as they begin to change color. Reflect on how God's love remains beautiful and constant, even as life changes around you.

Pray:
Dear God, thank you for the first fall leaves that remind me of your love in the middle of change. Help me to see the beauty in every season of life and to trust in your unchanging love. Amen.

September 20th

God designed you to work hard, but also to rest. When you create space for rest, you can appreciate the wonder of God's creation.

Pursue Wonder:
If you've been overworking, take a break today. Spend time in prayer or enjoy a restful activity that recharges you. As you rest,

thank God for his provision and presence, and allow yourself to experience the wonder of simply being still before God.

Pray:
Dear God, help me to find balance in my work and rest. Teach me to embrace the wonder of rest as a gift from you, and help me to trust that you provide for my every need. Amen.

SEPTEMBER 21ST

When you release the pressure to be perfect, you can rest in God's perfect love and enjoy the wonder of simply being God's child.

Pursue Wonder:
Striving for perfection can be exhausting and prevent you from seeing the wonder of God's grace. Reflect on an area of your life where you've been striving for perfection. Ask God to help you let go of the need to be flawless and instead embrace his grace. As you release perfectionism, notice how much more joy and wonder you find, even in life's imperfections. God's strength is made perfect in your weakness.

Pray:
Dear God, help me to let go of the need to be perfect and to trust in your grace. Open my heart to the wonder of living in the freedom of your love, and help me to embrace my imperfections with joy. Amen.

September 22nd

God is doing something new and wonderful in your life as the new season of fall begins.

Pursue Wonder:
As the fall season starts, consider what you hope God may do in your life this fall. Pray about it all, inviting God to bring the best to you in each of those situations.

Pray:
Dear God, thank you for the transition to this new season. Please bring wonder into my life this fall. Thank you, wonderful God. Amen.

September 23rd

When you unplug and engage with life more fully, you open yourself to the awe of God's creation and presence.

Pursue Wonder:
Constant screen time can desensitize you to the wonders of the world God has placed around you. Take a break from your phone, computer, or TV for a set period of time today. Use that time to connect with nature, pray, or spend time with friends and family. As you step away from screens, notice the wonderful details of the world around you that you can see now that you're paying closer attention.

Pray:

Dear God, help me to be mindful of how much time I spend on screens. Give me the strength to disconnect from distractions so I can be more aware of your wonders that surround me each day. Amen.

SEPTEMBER 24TH

When you turn to God instead of alcohol for peace when you're stressed, you can experience a greater sense of wonder in your life.

Pursue Wonder:

If you find yourself using alcohol to unwind or escape, take a step back and ask God to be your source of comfort instead. Spend time in prayer or go for a walk, inviting God into your need for rest and restoration. As you let go of habits that numb you, you'll discover a deeper sense of wonder in God's presence.

Pray:

Dear God, help me to turn to you instead of unhealthy habits when I need peace and comfort. Give me the strength to release anything that numbs me to your wonder, and help me live with a clear heart and mind. Amen.

SEPTEMBER 25TH

When you seek satisfaction from God instead of food, you can experience a deeper connection to God and his wonderful work in your life.

Pursue Wonder:

Turning to unhealthy foods for comfort can dull your sense of wonder for the good things God provides. Be mindful of how you approach food today. Instead of reaching for unhealthy snacks to soothe stress or boredom, pray and ask God to fill your heart with peace. As you nurture your body with healthy choices, you open yourself to experience God's wonder through both physical and spiritual nourishment.

Pray:

Dear God, please help me to honor you by taking care of my body and making wise choices about what I eat. Teach me to seek comfort in you rather than in unhealthy habits. May I experience your wonder through the health and strength you give me. Amen.

September 26th

When you seek purity and connection with God instead of through pornography, you can experience the fullness of God's wonderful love.

Pursue Wonder:

Pornography promises pleasure but leaves your soul feeling empty and disconnected from God's wonder. If pornography has been a struggle, know that God offers healing and grace. Ask God today to renew your mind and heart, leading you away from harmful habits and toward his love. As you walk in purity, you open yourself to a richer experience of God's wonder in relationships, love, and life itself.

Pray:

Dear God, cleanse my heart and mind from anything that dulls my sensitivity to your wonder. Help me to walk in purity and experience the joy and fulfillment that comes from being fully connected to you. Amen.

September 27th

God can fill you with wondrous peace as you breathe deeply and intentionally.

Pursue Wonder:

When stress weighs you down, one of the simplest yet most powerful ways to recenter yourself is through intentional breathing. Today, practice deep breathing as a form of prayer and stress relief. Inhale deeply, imagining God's peace filling you. Then exhale, letting go of your burdens. As you slow down and focus on your breath, you'll begin to notice the wonder of God's peace within you.

Pray:

Dear God, please breathe your peace into me today. As I focus on my breath, help me release my stress and experience the wonder of your presence within me. Amen.

September 28th

Simplifying your schedule creates space for you to slow down, reflect, and appreciate the wonder of the moments you may otherwise rush through.

Pursue Wonder:
    Busyness can block your awareness of God's work. Look at your schedule today and ask yourself: "What can I let go of to make room for God's wonder?" Prioritize rest, prayer, and time to enjoy the present moment. By simplifying, you'll discover new opportunities to marvel at God's work in the world around you.

Pray:
    Dear God, help me to declutter my life and make space for to notice your wonder. Show me how to let go of unnecessary busyness and be present to fully experience each awe-inspiring moment. Amen.

September 29th

Walking in nature is a powerful way to relieve stress and reconnect with God in ways that reveal wonder all around you.

Pursue Wonder:
    Step outside today and take a walk in nature. Pay attention to the sights, sounds, and smells of the world around you – the wind in the trees, the birds chirping, or the warmth of the sun. Let the beauty of creation remind you of the Creator's presence and fill you with awe.

Pray:

Dear God, thank you for the gift of nature and the wonder of how everything in your creation reflects something wonderful about you. As I walk in your creation today, help me release my stress and open my heart to the wonders you've placed all around me. Thank you, God. Amen.

September 30th

Stress often comes from trying to control something, but peace and wonder come from surrendering to God.

Pursue Wonder:

Trusting God allows you to experience the freedom of letting go and resting in his perfect plans for you. Reflect on an area of your life where you're feeling stressed because you're trying to control the outcome. Release it to God in prayer. As you surrender, trust that God's plans are higher than yours, and be open to the wonder of what God will do when you let go.

Pray:

Dear God, I surrender my need for control to you. Help me trust in your wisdom and timing, and fill me with wonder as I see how you work all things together for good. Amen.

OCTOBER

October 1st

The vibrant colors of fall can remind you of God's creative power.

Pursue Wonder:
 Take a walk today and admire the vibrant fall colors. Reflect on how God's creative power is displayed in nature and in your life.

Pray:
 Dear God, thank you for the vibrant colors of October. Help me to see your wonderful creative power at work in the world around me and in my life. Amen.

October 2nd

Experiencing joy through laughter lightens your heart and helps you notice wonder in fresh ways.

Pursue Wonder:
 Laughter is a powerful stress reliever, and it's also a gift from God. Find time today to laugh. Watch something funny, share jokes with friends, or recall a joyful memory. As you laugh, notice how your stress fades and how God's joy fills you with a sense of wonder.

Pray:
 Dear God, thank you for the gifts of laughter and joy. Help me to

see the wonder of your work even in the lighthearted moments of life and to release my stress through the joy you provide. Amen.

OCTOBER 3RD

When you trust in God's stability, you can face life's transitions with confidence and marvel at everything new that God is unfolding in your life.

Pursue Wonder:
    Change can be unsettling, but God is unchanging. If you're facing change today, reflect on God's constant presence in your life. Embrace the possibilities that come with change, trusting that God is guiding you toward wonderful opportunities for growth.

Pray:
    Dear God, please help me to embrace change and trust in your unchanging nature. Open my eyes to the new kinds of wonder you are unfolding in my life through this season of transition. Amen.

OCTOBER 4TH

Falling leaves teach you to let go of what you no longer need, freeing up more time and energy for you to experience God's wonder.

Pursue Wonder:
    Watch leaves as they fall from the trees around you. Consider

how God's wisdom teaches you to let go of whatever you no longer need in your life.

Pray:

Dear God, thank you for the wisdom that teaches me to let go of what no longer serves me well. Help me to release what I need to let go of in order to experience more wonder in my life. Amen.

October 5th

As you quiet your mind and let go of distractions through centering prayer, you can experience the wonder of simply being with God.

Pursue Wonder:

Centering prayer is a contemplative practice that helps you focus on God's presence in the depths of your soul. Practice centering prayer by choosing a sacred word or phrase, such as "peace" or "God is love." Sit in silence and repeat your chosen word or phrase whenever your mind begins to wander. In this quiet space, you can experience the wonder of God's peace filling your heart.

Pray:

Dear God, as I quiet my heart and focus on your presence, help me to rest in the wonder of simply being with you. May I find peace and renewal in your presence. Amen.

October 6th

God invites you to bring your requests to him in prayer, and when you do so, you can experience the wonder of God's provision and love.

Pursue Wonder:
Take time today to present your requests to God, no matter how big or small they may seem. As you lay them before God in prayer, remember that God delights in caring for you. Trust that God is already working on your behalf, and let the wonder of God's love fill your heart.

Pray:
Dear God, as I bring my requests before you today, I trust in your goodness and love. Help me to rest in the wonder of your care and provision as I place my needs in your hands. Amen.

October 7th

Writing your prayers down creates a powerful connection with God. Through prayer journaling, you can see the wonder of God at work as you document your thoughts, needs, and praises.

Pursue Wonder:
Take time today to write a prayer in a journal. Express your heart fully to God on paper and plan to look back over past entries to see how God has been answering your prayers. As you reflect on God's faithfulness, you'll be filled with wonder at how God moves in your life over time.

Pray:

Dear God, help me to see your wonder as I journal my prayers. Open my eyes to the wonderful ways you are working in my life. Amen.

October 8th

Praying with others allows you to experience the wonderful power of community as you seek God's will together.

Pursue Wonder:

Join with others in prayer today, either in person or virtually. As you pray together, notice how God's presence feels even stronger when you're united in purpose. Trust that God hears your collective prayers and be open to the wonder of what God may do through the power of unity.

Pray:

Dear God, thank you for the gift of community. Help me to experience your wonder as I join with others in prayer and trust that you are present with us. Thank you, our loving God. Amen.

October 9th

Technology can be a source of distraction and stress, but unplugging from it allows you to experience more of God's wonder in the world around you.

Pursue Wonder:

Set aside some time today to unplug from technology. When you step away from screens, you create space for real-life connection and reflection. Instead of reaching for your phone, spend that time in prayer, reading, or simply observing the world around you. Let the quiet of being "unplugged" open your heart to God's presence and help you release the stress of constant digital noise.

Pray:

Dear God, help me to disconnect from distractions today and reconnect with you. Show me the wonder of living free from the stress of technology, and open my heart to what you want to show me. Amen.

October 10th

When you ask God for guidance, you open yourself to the wonder of perceiving God's wisdom.

Pursue Wonder:

If you're facing a decision today, take time to ask God for guidance. As you pray, listen for God's voice and trust that he will lead you in the right direction. Let go of anxiety and open your heart to the wonder of the message God shares with you.

Pray:

Dear God, I need your guidance about the situations that are on my mind today. I trust that you will lead me on the right path. Please fill me with wonder as I witness how you work in my life. Amen.

OCTOBER 11TH

Meditating on God's promises allows you to dwell on God's faithfulness and feel reassured by the wonder of God's constant loving care for you.

Pursue Wonder:
Choose a promise from the Bible and meditate on it today. For example, consider Philippians 4:19: "My God will meet all your needs according to the riches of his glory in Christ Jesus." Reflect on how this promise relates to your life and notice how it fills you with wonder at God's abundant provision.

Pray:
Dear God, thank you for the promises you've made to me. As I meditate on your Word, help me to trust in your faithfulness and experience the wonder of your care for me. Amen.

OCTOBER 12TH

The wondrous beauty of fall leaves, which only lasts briefly, reminds you celebrate the fleeting moments of life.

Pursue Wonder:
Today, take time to admire the beauty of fall leaves. Reflect on how their fleeting beauty reminds you to celebrate the joyful moments of life as they pass by quickly.

Pray:

Dear God, thank you for the beauty of fall leaves that reminds me to celebrate life's joyful moments. Help me to cherish the time you have given me. Amen.

October 13th

When you exercise, you can release tension and experience the wonder of how God has designed your body to function and thrive.

Pursue Wonder:

Exercise is a natural stress reliever, and it's also a way to honor God by caring for your body. Take time for physical activity today, such as a gym workout, a walk, or stretching exercises. As you move, focus on the strength and flexibility God has given you. Notice how physical activity helps release stress and how it can be a time to reflect on God's wonderful design for your body.

Pray:

Dear God, thank you for the ability to move and use my body. Help me to care for this wonderful body you've given me and to find stress relief and inspiration through physical exercise. Amen.

October 14th

In times of uncertainty or stress, prayer can bring the wonder of God's peace into your life – calming your spirit and bringing you into alignment with God's perfect will.

Pursue Wonder:

If you're feeling anxious today, bring your worries to God in prayer. Ask God to fill your heart with his peace. As you release your fears to God, notice how the wonder of God's peace can calm even the most stressful situations.

Pray:

Dear God, I'm anxious about the situations on my mind today, but I'm bringing those anxieties to you. Please fill me with your peace and help me to trust in your care. Thank you for letting me experience the wonder of your calming presence. Amen.

October 15th

When you choose to release your anxieties to God, you clear space for trust and awe to fill your heart.

Pursue Wonder:

Worry clouds your ability to see the wonder of God at work. Today, consciously let go of a worry that has been weighing on your mind. Write it down and give it to God in prayer. Instead of focusing on the "what-ifs," notice the ways God is already providing for you. Trust God with the unknown, and see the wonder in God's faithfulness.

Pray:

Dear God, I release my worries into your hands. Thank you for providing for me. Help me to recognize the wonder of your care for me, even in the smallest details of my life. Amen.

October 16th

When you see yourself through God's eyes, you begin to experience the wonder of your identity as one of God's beloved children – someone who is chosen, valued, and loved.

Pursue Wonder:
Insecurity makes you feel small, but God's love reveals your true worth. When you feel insecure today, pause and remind yourself of God's truth about you. Reflect on Psalm 139:14: "I praise you because I am fearfully and wonderfully made." Let those words affirm your worth, and experience the wonder of being fully known and fully loved by God.

Pray:
Dear God, please help me to see myself as you see me. In moments of insecurity, remind me of my worth in your eyes and fill me with wonder at the love you have for me. Amen.

October 17th

Through prayer, you can explore the wondrous depths of God's infinite wisdom.

Pursue Wonder:
Prayer is not only about asking for what you need, but also seeking God's wisdom. As you pray today, focus on asking God to open your mind and heart to his wisdom. Reflect and allow yourself

to ponder questions you may not fully understand. Ask God to guide your thoughts with discernment and clarity. Notice how God reveals the wonder of his design in ways that may surprise you.

Pray:
　　Dear God, give me the wisdom to see your wonder in every situation, even in the mysteries of life. Help me seek your truth and trust in your divine understanding as you reveal your wisdom. Thank you, my wise God. Amen.

October 18th

Praying in nature can draw you into a deeper sense of God's wonder.

Pursue Wonder:
　　Take your prayer time outside today, such as on a walk or sitting quietly in a park. Surrounded by God's creation, you can feel God's presence vividly as you pray. Notice the beauty of the natural world around you and reflect on how it reveals God's creative power and love. Let God's creation inspire awe in you.

Pray:
　　Dear God, thank you for the beauty of your creation. As I pray in nature today, help me to see your wonderful work all around me and be filled with awe by your presence. Amen.

October 19th

The Bible is filled with divine mysteries.

Pursue Wonder:
When you approach the Bible with discernment, the Holy Spirit illuminates its mysteries, deepening your understanding and awe. Choose a biblical passage that you find challenging or mysterious. Spend time meditating on it, asking God to reveal its meaning to you. As God opens your eyes to the wonder of his Word, reflect on how the truth within it applies to your life.

Pray:
God, your Word is full of mysteries that invite me into deeper understanding. Give me the discernment to see the wonder in your teachings and the wisdom to apply them to my life. Amen.

October 20th

Creativity is a gift from God, and using art in prayer can be a powerful way to connect with God.

Pursue Wonder:
Spend time today creating art as a form of prayer. You can express your prayers visually – such as through drawing, painting, or building with modeling clay – and experience the wonder of creativity as a form of worship. Let your creativity flow as an expression of your love and worship of God. As you create, meditate on how God, the ultimate Creator, has given you the ability to reflect his image through your own creativity.

Pray:

Dear God, thank you for the gift of creativity. Help me to use my artistic expression as a way to connect with you and experience the wonder of worship through art. Amen.

October 21st

Reflecting on the beauty of creation through prayer allows you to connect deeply with God, the Creator of all.

Pursue Wonder:

Go outside or sit near a window today, and meditate on the beauty of God's creation. Let each aspect of nature – the sky, trees, rocks, or even the smallest insect – remind you of God's wonderful power and care for every detail.

Pray:

Dear God, as I look at your creation, I'm in awe of your creativity and power. Open my eyes to see the wonder of your creation in new and deeper ways. Amen.

October 22nd

In God's hands, even failure becomes an opportunity for growth and wonder.

Pursue Wonder:

The fear of failure can hold you back from fully embracing God's plans for you. So, step out in faith today, even if you're afraid of failing. Trust that God will guide you through success and setbacks alike. Each step is part of God's plan for your growth. Be open to learning and growing from every experience, with the confidence that God is with you and is working out good purposes for your life.

Pray:
Dear God, help me overcome the fear of failure. Give me the courage to step forward in faith, trusting that you will use both my successes and failures to reveal the wonder of your good purposes for me. Amen.

October 23rd

When you release anger and choose forgiveness, you open yourself to God's healing and experience God's awe-inspiring grace.

Pursue Wonder:
Anger can blind you to God's wonder, filling your heart with turmoil instead of peace. When you feel angry today, take a deep breath and bring your emotions to God. Ask for God's help to let go of anger and choose forgiveness. As you release your grip on bitterness, notice the wonder of how God's peace can fill your heart.

Pray:
Dear God, please help me let go of my anger and replace it with your peace. Teach me to forgive as you have forgiven me, and help me experience the wonder of your healing grace in my heart. Amen.

October 24th

Trusting God in the uncertainty opens your eyes to the wonder of God's perfect plans, even when you can't see the full picture.

Pursue Wonder:
　　The fear of the unknown can keep you stuck in worry, but God calls you to walk in faith. Take time today to reflect on an area of your life where you feel uncertain. Bring it before God in prayer, asking God to replace your fear with faith. As you trust God with the unknown, expect to see God's wonder as he guides you step by step.

Pray:
　　Dear God, help me trust you when the future is unclear. Replace my fear of the unknown with faith in your plans, and help me to marvel at the ways you lead me through life's uncertainties with love. Amen.

October 25th

The resilience of nature can point you to God's wonderful strength as it reminds you to persevere through life's challenges.

Pursue Wonder:
　　Notice how nature continues to thrive in any kind of weather. Reflect on how God's strength helps you to persevere through life's challenges and to remain steadfast in faith.

Pray:

Dear God, thank you for the strength that helps me persevere through life's challenges. Help me to trust in your power and to remain steadfast in faith, no matter what comes my way. Amen.

October 26th

When you release anxiety about relationships to God, you open yourself to the wonder of deeper, healthier connections rooted in love.

Pursue Wonder:

God calls you to love without fear. If you're feeling anxious about a relationship today, take it to God in prayer. Ask God to help you let go of fear and trust him with the outcome. As you do, watch for the wonder of how God can help you let go of unhealthy relationships and strengthen your healthy relationships with his love.

Pray:

Dear God, help me release my anxiety in relationships and trust you with my connections. Fill my heart with your love and grace so I can experience the wonder of healthy, life-giving relationships. Amen.

October 27th

The harvest moon can remind you of God's faithfulness in every season.

Pursue Wonder:

Look for the harvest moon tonight, and enjoy its bright glow. Reflect on how its light reminds you of God's faithfulness in every season, providing for your needs and guiding you through the darkness.

Pray:

Dear God, thank you for the harvest moon that reminds me of your provision. Help me to trust in your faithfulness and to rely on your care through every season of life. Amen.

October 28th

When you release the need to be perfect and accept God's love as you are, you open yourself to the wonder of God's unconditional love and mercy.

Pursue Wonder:

Perfectionism can be paralyzing, preventing you from fully experiencing God's grace. Today, choose to let go of the pressure to be perfect. Accept that God loves you just as you are, with all your flaws and imperfections. Allow this truth to fill you with the wonder of God's grace, and let go of striving for perfection.

Pray:

Dear God, I release my need to be perfect and rest in the truth of your love. Help me experience the wonder of your grace. Please meet me where I am and transform me in ways only you can. Amen.

October 29th

When you trust in God's strength rather than your own, you begin to see the wonder of what God can accomplish through you.

Pursue Wonder:
Self-doubt can rob you of confidence, but God equips you for every good work. Whenever self-doubt creeps in today, pause and remember Philippians 4:13: "I can do all things through Christ who strengthens me." Trust that God will empower you, and be open to the wonder of how God's strength can work through you.

Pray:
Dear God, please help me to overcome self-doubt by trusting in your strength. Show me the wonder of what you can do through me, even when I feel inadequate. Amen.

October 30th

Knowing that you are secure in God's love allows you to live freely – without fear – and embrace the wonder of who God has made you to be.

Pursue Wonder:
The fear of rejection can limit you, but God has already accepted you completely. If you're holding back from something out of fear of rejection, take a step forward today. Remember that God's love is constant and unconditional. Embrace the wonder of being fully

accepted by God, and let that truth give you the courage to move forward.

Pray:
Dear God, remind me that I am fully accepted by you, no matter what. Help me to overcome the fear of rejection and live confidently in the wonder of your love. Amen.

October 31st

When you trust in God's presence, even when you're afraid, you can experience the peace that comes from knowing God is always in control.

Pursue Wonder:
Fear often keeps you from seeing the fullness of God's wonder in your life. Take time today to reflect on any fears or worries that are weighing you down. Surrender them to God in prayer, trusting in God's good plans. As you release those burdens, allow yourself to feel lighter and more open to experiencing God's wonder in new and unexpected ways. Trust that God is with you in every step and that God's love casts out all fear.

Pray:
Dear God, help me to let go of my fears and worries while trusting you to do what's best in those situations. Open my heart to see your wonder even when I feel afraid, and fill me with the confidence that you are always in control. Amen.

NOVEMBER

November 1st

Gratitude shifts your focus from stress to wonder.

Pursue Wonder:
When you take time to thank God for the blessings he pours into your life, you can remember God's goodness and feel awe for God's generous provision. Start a gratitude list today. Write down three things you're thankful for, no matter how simple they are. A thankful heart will help you sense God's presence with you. As you practice gratitude, watch how your stress begins to melt away and wonder takes its place.

Pray:
Dear God, thank you for all you have given me. As I practice gratitude today, help me to see the wonder in every blessing and to let go of the stress that keeps me from fully appreciating your gifts. Amen.

November 2nd

Gratitude shifts your focus from fear to faith.

Pursue Wonder:
When you thank God for your blessings, your heart opens to the wonder of how God is working in your life – even in scary situations. Whenever fear arises today, counter it with a moment of gratitude. Write down or speak aloud the things you are thankful for. As you practice gratitude, allow the fear to fade and let wonder fill its place.

Gratitude is a powerful reminder of God's continual presence and provision.

Pray:
 Dear God, thank you for the many blessings you have poured into my life. When fear tries to take hold, help me to focus on your goodness and to live in the wonder of your faithful care. Amen.

November 3rd

Keeping a gratitude journal can help you see God's answers to your prayers over time.

Pursue Wonder:
 Start a habit of writing down something you're grateful for, every single day, in a gratitude journal. Take special note of how God is working to answer your prayers. Whenever you need encouragement or inspiration, read past entries to remind yourself of God's wondrous work in your life.

Pray:
 Dear God, thank you for always answering my prayers – in the best timing and ways – because of your wonderful love for me. I love you, God. Amen.

November 4th

The bare branches of November trees reflect God's wisdom by teaching you to find wonderful beauty in simplicity.

Pursue Wonder:
Watch the trees as they shed their leaves. Reflect on how God's wisdom teaches you to find beauty in simplicity, while God's creation around you simplifies for the upcoming winter season.

Pray:
Dear God, thank you for the beauty in simplicity that November reveals. Help me to appreciate the simple things in life and to see your wonder in every detail. Amen.

November 5th

God's grace is a boundless gift that fills life with wonder.

Pursue Wonder:
Gratitude for God's unmerited favor reminds you of how deeply you are loved and how wondrous God's mercy is as it renews you each day. Spend time today meditating on God's grace in your life. Think about the forgiveness, blessings, and second chances God has given you. Let gratitude for God's grace fill your heart and inspire you to live with more wonder and joy.

Pray:
Dear God, thank you for the gift of your grace. I'm amazed by the

mercy and love you show me every day. Help me live in gratitude for your grace and share that grace with others. Amen.

November 6th

When you reflect on God's faithfulness in your life, you can experience wonder.

Pursue Wonder:
    God's consistent care and guidance through every season of life remind you of his loving presence with you. Today, recall specific ways God has been faithful in your life. Whether it's answered prayers, unexpected blessings, or provision in hard times, thank God for the ways he has come through for you. Let the wonder of God's faithfulness draw you closer to him.

Pray:
    Dear God, you have been so faithful to me in countless ways. Thank you for your unwavering love and care. Fill my heart with gratitude and wonder as I reflect on your faithfulness. Amen.

November 7th

Cultivating gratitude for your relationships opens your heart to the wonder of how God connects us to one another in meaningful ways.

Pursue Wonder:

The people in your life are gifts from God. Think of the people who have made a positive impact on your life. Reach out to one or two of them today with a word of thanks, either in person or through a message. As you express gratitude, notice how the wonder of connection brings more joy into your relationships.

Pray:
Dear God, thank you for the people you have placed in my life. I'm grateful for the love, support, and friendship they bring. Help me to see your wonder in the connections you've woven into my life. Amen.

November 8th

Meditating on God's creation reveals the wonder of God's artistry and creativity.

Pursue Wonder:
From the majesty of mountains to the intricate beauty of a flower, nature reflects the glory of God's character. Meditate on a part of God's creation today. Whether it's a tree outside your window or the sky above, focus on its beauty and consider what it reveals about God's nature. Let the wonder of God's handiwork inspire you with awe.

Pray:
Dear God, as I meditate on the beauty of your creation, help me to see the wonder of your power and creativity. May the world around me continually point me back to you. Amen.

November 9th

Praying through the Bible allows you to align your heart with God's Word and experience the wonder of God's promises.

Pursue Wonder:
As you declare God's truth in your prayers, you invite God's power and wisdom into your life. Choose a verse or passage from the Bible and incorporate it into your prayers today. For example, you might pray Psalm 23: "Lord, thank you for being my shepherd, for guiding and comforting me." As you pray through the verse or passage you chose, let its truths fill your heart with wonder at God's faithfulness.

Pray:
Dear God, thank you for the gift of your Word. As I pray about it, please help me to stand on your promises and experience the wonder of your unchanging truth. Amen.

November 10th

Gratitude for your spiritual growth helps you see the wonder of how God works within you, transforming your soul over time to be holy.

Pursue Wonder:
Each step of spiritual growth you go through shows the depth of God's love for you. Take time to reflect on how you've grown spiritually in recent months or years. Consider the areas where God has

stretched you and given you new insights or strengths. Thank God for the ways he is shaping your character, and marvel at the wonder of God's ongoing work in your life.

Pray:
　　Dear God, thank you for the ways you've helped me grow spiritually. I'm in awe of how you continually work within me, molding me into who you've called me to be. Amen.

November 11th

When you take time to rest and express gratitude for it, you experience the wonder of God's peace and renewal.

Pursue Wonder:
　　Rest is a precious gift that refreshes both body and soul. Today, carve out time to rest, even if it's just a few quiet moments. As you rest, thank God for this time to recharge and reflect on how rest itself is a gift that reveals God's care for your well-being. Embrace the wonder of resting in God's peace.

Pray:
　　Dear God, thank you for the gift of rest. In a busy world, I'm grateful for moments to slow down and be renewed by your peace. Help me to embrace rest as a reflection of your love for me. Amen.

November 12th

When you slow down to eat mindfully, you experience not only the nourishment of food but also the wonder of God's provision.

Pursue Wonder:

Eating with gratitude can reduce stress and heighten your awareness of God's goodness. At your next meal, pause before you eat. Offer a prayer of thanks and pay attention to the flavors, textures, and smells of the food. Eat slowly, savoring each bite, and reflect on how God has provided for your physical and spiritual nourishment.

Pray:

Dear God, thank you for providing everything I need. As I eat today, help me to be mindful of the wonder of your care for me. Amen.

November 13th

God's strength is like the roots of a tree, grounding you in faith and helping you to stand strong in the face of challenges.

Pursue Wonder:

Look at the roots of a tree and consider how those roots anchor the tree to the ground. Reflect on how God's strength grounds you in faith, helping you to stand strong through life's challenges.

Pray:

Dear God, thank you for the strength that grounds me in faith.

Help me to stand strong in your power, no matter what challenges I face. Amen.

November 14th

When you step away from your work for a break, you open yourself to the wonder of God's presence in rest and renewal.

Pursue Wonder:
Taking breaks isn't just about rest; it's about giving your mind and spirit the space to recharge. Take intentional breaks throughout your day. Whether it's a short walk, a few moments of prayer, or simply sitting in stillness, let those breaks be times of reconnecting with God. As you rest, you'll find that stress fades, and you're more attuned to the wonder of God's sustaining power.

Pray:
Dear God, help me to remember the importance of taking breaks to rest in you. As I pause today, refresh my spirit and fill me with wonder at how you renew me when I rest in your presence. Amen.

November 15th

Watching animals gather food for the upcoming winter can remind you to trust God to care for your own needs.

Pursue Wonder:

Notice how animals gather food for the winter. Reflect on how God provides for your needs, just as he cares for all of creation. Choose to trust God to provide whatever you need for your own future.

Pray:
Dear God, thank you for the many ways you care for my needs every day. I trust you to provide for all the needs on my mind. Please help me to rely on your care through every season of life. Amen.

November 16th

Exploring God's mysteries reveals awe-inspiring glimpses of God that can draw you into a deeper relationship with him.

Pursue Wonder:
Dedicate time today to meditate on a passage of the Bible that speaks about the mystery of God's ways, like Romans 11:33, which begins: "Oh, the depth of the riches of the wisdom and knowledge of God!...". As you reflect, ask for discernment and let the wonder of God's infinite wisdom fill your heart.

Pray:
Dear God, I recognize that I can't fully comprehend your ways, but thank you for the mysteries that invite me to know you more deeply. Please give me discernment as I seek to explore your wonder. Amen.

November 17th

Creation is full of mysteries that reflect the Creator's majesty and creativity.

Pursue Wonder:
From the depths of the ocean to the farthest reaches of the universe, every part of creation tells a story of God's wondrous power and design. Take time today to research a mystery in nature – such as the migration of birds, the life cycle of a butterfly, or the vastness of space. As you explore, allow the intricacy and beauty of creation to deepen your awe of God, the Creator.

Pray:
Dear God, your creation is filled with wonders I can barely comprehend. Help me to approach these mysteries with curiosity and discernment, so that I can see your work in everything. Amen.

November 18th

Although you may not always understand why things happen when they do, trusting in God's timing can open your eyes to wonder.

Pursue Wonder:
One of the greatest mysteries is God's timing – how God works all things together according to his perfect plan. Reflect on a situation in your life where you've questioned God's timing. Ask God for discernment and patience as you trust God's plan. Consider how

previous delays or detours have led to unexpected blessings, and find wonder in how God orchestrates every detail.

Pray:
Dear God, help me trust your timing, even when I don't understand it. Give me the discernment to recognize the ways you are working in my life, and fill me with wonder as I do. Amen.

November 19th

As you pray, the Holy Spirit reveals mysteries and truths that draw you closer to God's purposes for your life.

Pursue Wonder:
God invites you into a deeper understanding of his will and wonder through prayer. Today, set aside extra time for prayer. Ask God to reveal more of his will for your life and his presence in the world around you. Approach God with a heart of curiosity and openness, trusting that God will unveil the wonders of his plans in the best timing.

Pray:
Dear God, as I pray, I want to understand more of the mysteries of your will. Please give me discernment and help me to trust in the ways you reveal yourself. Let me experience the wonder of being in your presence and knowing you more. Amen.

November 20th

God's plans often unfold in ways you could never have anticipated.

Pursue Wonder:
Although God's plans may seem mysterious or even unclear at times, they are always full of purpose and wonder as they unfold. Look back on a time in your life when you couldn't see the full picture, but later saw how God's plan unfolded in a beautiful way. Reflect on how that mystery was revealed and thank God for the wonder of his plans that are greater than you anticipated.

Pray:
Dear God, your plans are a mystery that unfolds with beauty and purpose. Help me to trust you even when I can't see the whole picture, and to stand in awe as your wonder is revealed in my life. Amen.

November 21st

Through faith, you can experience the deep wonder of God's presence and power in your life.

Pursue Wonder:
Faith itself is a mystery – believing in what you can't see, and trusting in what you can't fully understand. Today, reflect on the mystery of faith. Take a step of faith in an area where you've been hesitant, trusting that God will meet you in that place of uncertainty. As you do, be open to experiencing the wonder that comes when you place your trust in God.

Pray:

Dear God, faith is such a beautiful mystery. Help me to trust you more deeply and to walk by faith, not by sight. Fill me with wonder as I experience your presence and power in my life. Amen.

November 22nd

The wonderful abundance of God's blessings reminds you to share what you have with others.

Pursue Wonder:

Consider the abundance of blessings that God has given you in all areas of your life. Let your gratitude for those blessings motivate you to share your blessings with others.

Pray:

Dear God, thank you for the abundance of blessings you have given me. Please help me to share what I have with others and to reflect your generosity in the world. Amen.

November 23rd

Human relationships can be complex in ways that reveal God's wonder.

Pursue Wonder:

When you approach relationships with love, discernment, and grace, you see the wonder of how God connects us to one another in beautiful ways. Reflect on the relationships in your life and how God has used them to shape and bless you. Consider one person you may need to reconnect with or show extra grace to, and take a step toward strengthening that relationship today. See the wonder in how God weaves our lives together.

Pray:
Dear God, thank you for the gift of relationships and the wonder of human connection. Help me approach my relationships with discernment, love, and grace, so I can experience more of your presence through them. Amen.

November 24th

God's guidance is always available to those who seek it – and when you do, you experience the wonder of knowing that you are never alone in your decisions.

Pursue Wonder:
Think about a time when God's guidance led you in the right direction – such as through prayer, a Bible passage, or wise advice from another believer. Thank God for leading you, and trust that God will continue to guide you as you seek his guidance regularly.

Pray:
Dear God, thank you for guiding me every step of the way. I'm in awe of how you direct my life and give me the wisdom I need. Help

me to trust your guidance and live in the wonder of knowing you are always with me. Amen.

November 25th

Serving others is a powerful way to experience God's wonder.

Pursue Wonder:
By expressing gratitude for opportunities to serve, you can recognize how God is working through you to bless others. That reveals God's love and compassion in action. Look for an opportunity to serve someone today – such as through kind words or through a generous act. As you serve, marvel at the wonder of how God uses you to make a difference in other people's lives.

Pray:
Dear God, thank you for the opportunities you give me to serve others. I'm grateful for the ways you work through me to spread your love and care. Help me to see the wonder of your work in every way I serve. Amen.

November 26th

It's often something small yet significant that reveals God's wonder in everyday life – the warmth of the sun, a smile from a friend, or a delicious meal.

Pursue Wonder:
When you're grateful for small blessings, you open your eyes to the constant presence of God's goodness. Write down three small things you're thankful for today. As you reflect on these small blessings, notice how God's love is woven into the ordinary moments of your life. Let gratitude awaken wonder within you.

Pray:
Dear God, thank you for the small blessings that fill my life with joy and remind me of your care. Help me to notice and appreciate the wonder of these everyday gifts. Amen.

NOVEMBER 27TH

Gratitude unlocks the wonder of God's blessings – big and small alike.

Pursue Wonder:
When you approach God with a heart of gratitude, you open your eyes to the countless ways God is already at work in your life. Begin your prayers today by thanking God for specific blessings in your life. As you practice gratitude, you'll notice more and more of God's wonders.

Pray:
Dear God, thank you for your abundant blessings in my life. Help me to always be aware of the wonders you provide each day. Amen.

November 28th

Finding gratitude during difficult seasons is not easy, but it allows you to see God's wonder even in the middle of your challenges.

Pursue Wonder:

Gratitude opens your heart to the peace and hope that come from trusting that God is working through every challenge. Reflect on a current or past difficulty. As you do, ask God to show you where God has been at work, even when things were hard. Give thanks for the strength and growth God has brought through the challenge, and let this gratitude deepen your sense of wonder.

Pray:

Dear God, it's hard to feel grateful in difficult times, but I know you are with me even in the struggles. Help me to see your hand at work and to thank you for the strength, wisdom, and hope you bring. Amen.

November 29th

The more you reflect on the mystery of grace, the more you can experience the wonder of God's love.

Pursue Wonder:

God's grace is a mystery beyond human comprehension. We can't earn it or fully understand it, yet it's freely given. Spend time today meditating on the concept of grace. Thank God for the ways his grace has impacted your life, and reflect on how the mystery of unearned favor reveals God's deep love and care for you. Let this reflection fill you with wonder.

Pray:
Dear God, your grace is a mystery that leaves me in awe. Thank you for loving me so deeply and for extending grace even when I don't deserve it. Help me live in the wonder of your love every day. Amen.

November 30th

Gratitude in prayer opens your heart to seeing God's wonder in all circumstances.

Pursue Wonder:
As you pray today, focus solely on giving thanks. Pray specifically about every blessing that comes to your mind. Notice how gratitude shifts your perspective and helps you recognize God's wonder at work all around you.

Pray:
Dear God, thank you for the endless blessings you're constantly pouring into my life. May my heart overflow with gratitude, and may I never take for granted the wonder of your goodness in my life. Amen.

DECEMBER

December 1st

As December begins, God's love lights up the world as the first Christmas lights begin to shine in the darkness.

Pursue Wonder:
 Notice the Christmas lights that start to appear in your neighborhood. Reflect on how God's love shines in your life, even in the darkest of times.

Pray:
 Dear God, thank you for the light of your love that brightens the world. Help me to see your presence in the light that surrounds me and to share your love with others. Amen.

December 2nd

As you prepare your heart for Christmas, you can experience the wonder of God's promises fulfilled.

Pursue Wonder:
 Advent is a season of waiting and anticipation, reminding you of the wonder of when Jesus came to Earth to save the world. This Advent, take time each day to reflect on God's historical promises that the Savior would arrive at the determined time. Whether you light candles on an Advent wreath or read Bible passages about the birth of Jesus, allow your anticipation to deepen your sense of wonder at God's love and faithfulness.

Pray:

Dear God, thank you for the promise of Jesus' coming. Help me to embrace the wonder of this season with anticipation and joy, knowing that you are always faithful to your promises. Amen.

December 3rd

Sometimes, the greatest wonder comes in quiet moments, such as during silent prayer.

Pursue Wonder:

Silent prayer allows you to step away from distractions and focus entirely on God's presence. Set aside time today to pray without words. Sit in silence before God and open your heart to God's presence. Notice how God's peace and guidance come to you – not through noise, but through quiet yet powerful messages. This simple practice welcomes awe into your life as you rest in the knowledge that God knows what's on your heart, even when you can't find the words to articulate it.

Pray:

Dear God, teach me to be still before you. In the silence, let me hear your voice and feel your presence. May your wonder fill my soul in these quiet moments of prayer. Amen.

December 4th

You can celebrate the wonder God's peace in the Christmas carols you sing.

Pursue Wonder:
　Sing or listen to a Christmas carol today, focusing on the message of peace it brings. Reflect on how the birth of Jesus brings peace to you and to the world.

Pray:
　Dear God, thank you for the message of peace that Christmas carols highlight. Help me to carry this peace with me and to share it with others. Thank you, wonderful God. Amen.

December 5th

Intercessory prayer is a powerful way to experience the wonder of God's love at work.

Pursue Wonder:
　As you pray for others, you partner with God in his plans and purposes, and witness the wonder of God answering those prayers. Spend time in intercession today, lifting up the needs of other people to God. As you pray, reflect on the wonder of being part of God's work in the lives of those around you. Trust that God hears your prayers and is working in ways you can't yet see.

Pray:

Dear God, thank you for allowing me to participate in your work through intercessory prayer. Help me to see the wonder of how you move in the lives of others as I pray for them. Amen.

December 6th

No matter how difficult or dark life may feel at times, the wonder of God's light can point you toward hope.

Pursue Wonder:
As the days grow shorter in December, look for the beauty in the lights around you – such as an Advent candle or the glow of Christmas lights. Let each source of light remind you of the powerful truth that God sent his light into a dark world through the birth of Jesus. Celebrate the reality that Jesus is the Light of the World, shining hope into every corner of your life.

Pray:
Dear God, thank you for sending your light into the world through Jesus. Help me to see your light in the middle of the dark circumstances I face and to reflect that light to others during this Christmas season. Amen.

December 7th

You can experience significant wonder in the simple pleasures of the Christmas season.

Pursue Wonder:

Enjoy a simple pleasure today, such as eating a Christmas cookie or singing along to a favorite Christmas carol. Consider how these simple activities are gifts from God that can inspire you in powerful ways.

Pray:

Dear God, thank you for the simple pleasures that inspire me with awe during this season. Help me to cherish the joy you bring into my life during every season. Amen.

December 8th

Kind words and actions point people to the wonder of God's love, which flows through you as you choose kindness.

Pursue Wonder:

Find a way to spread kindness this Christmas season – such as by donating to a local charity, giving time to a neighbor, or encouraging someone who is struggling. Let your kindness reflect the wonder of God's love.

Pray:

Dear God, thank you for how kindness reveals the wonder of your love. Help me to intentionally choose kindness day by day. Amen.

December 9th

God reveals the wonder of his love as you give gifts to the people you love.

Pursue Wonder:

The Christmas season invites you to reflect on the greatest gift of all: Jesus Christ, the world's Savior. In response, you can share God's love by giving generously to others. As you shop for or make Christmas gifts, reflect on how each gift is a symbol of the love God has shown through the ultimate gift of Jesus. Enjoy the wonder of how God's love flows through your life into other people's lives as you bless them with gifts.

Pray:

Dear God, thank you for the gift of Jesus – the most wonderful expression of your love. Help me to give gifts that reflect your love and to remember the true meaning of this season. Amen.

December 10th

Advent candle flames remind you of the awe-inspiring light that Jesus brings into the world.

Pursue Wonder:

Light an Advent candle today. Reflect on how the flame represents Jesus, the Light of the World, who shines brightly in the world's darkness. As you gaze into the candle, let feelings of awe wash over you.

Pray:
Dear God, thank you for the ultimate light of hope that you bring into our dark world through Jesus. Please shine Jesus' light through my life so people who are looking for hope can see it and discover hope through relationships with you. Amen.

December 11th

Christmas music fills you with joy and wonder as it reminds you of the miracle of Jesus' birth.

Pursue Wonder:
Through Christmas songs, you can express gratitude for God's amazing love and share in the celebration of God's presence with you. This Christmas, enjoy listening to your favorite carols. Sing along, paying attention to the lyrics and allowing their message to fill your heart with the wonder of Jesus' birth. Let the music draw you closer to God in worship.

Pray:
Dear God, thank you for the gift of music that helps me celebrate the birth of Jesus. As I listen to Christmas carols this season, may I feel the wonder of your presence and rejoice in the gift of your son Jesus. Amen.

December 12th

You can discover the wonder of God's strength through Mary, who faithfully trusted in God's plan even when she couldn't see the outcome.

Pursue Wonder:
Read the Christmas story in the Bible. Reflect on Mary's faith and strength as she accepted God's plan for her life. Consider how you can trust in God's plan for you, even when the future is uncertain.

Pray:
Dear God, thank you for the wonderful example of Mary's faith and strength. Help me to trust in your plan for my life, even when I don't know what lies ahead. Amen.

December 13th

God's love is like the wondrous star that guided the wise men, since it leads you to the Savior who brings light to your life.

Pursue Wonder:
Look at the stars tonight, if the sky is clear where you live. Consider how the star of Bethlehem led the wise men to Jesus, and how God's love guides you to the Savior who brings light into your life.

Pray:

Dear God, thank you for guiding me to Jesus, the Light of the World. Help me to follow your leading and to find my way to the Savior who brings hope and love into my life. Amen.

December 14th

The Christmas season is filled with symbols that point you back to the wonder of God's story.

Pursue Wonder:

Take time today to notice the Christmas symbols around you – such as the evergreen tree symbolizing eternal life, the star representing the light of hope, and the gifts reminding you of the ultimate gift of Jesus. Reflect on the deeper meaning behind them and how each one points back to the wonder of God's love and plan for redemption. Let these symbols draw you into a deeper appreciation of the true meaning of Christmas.

Pray:

Dear God, thank you for the symbols of Christmas that remind me of your love and the miracle of Jesus' birth. Help me to see the wonder in each one and to keep my focus on the true meaning of this season. Amen.

December 15th

The laughter of children can remind you to approach Christmas with childlike wonder.

Pursue Wonder:

Spend time with children today, or remember the joy of Christmas from your own childhood. Consider how embracing childlike wonder as an adult this Christmas can draw you closer to God.

Pray:

Dear God, thank you for the joy of children that reminds me to approach Christmas with wonder. Help me to see the world through their eyes and to embrace the excitement of this season with pure wonder. Amen.

December 16th

You can discover the wonder of God's strength in the journey of the shepherds, who went to see the newborn King despite their fears.

Pursue Wonder:

Think about the shepherds who left everything to find Jesus on the first Christmas. Reflect on how their journey required strength and courage, and how God can give you the strength to follow his call in your own life.

Pray:

Dear God, thank you for the strength you gave the shepherds to seek out the newborn King. Help me to follow your call in my life with the same courage and trust in you. Amen.

December 17th

It's often in moments of silence and stillness that you can experience the wonder of God's presence most deeply.

Pursue Wonder:
    It's easy to get caught up in the noise and distractions of the busy Christmas season. Find time for silence and stillness today. Set aside some time to meditate on the miracle of Jesus' birth. In the silence, ask God to reveal his wonder to you in a fresh way and to fill your heart with peace.

Pray:
    Dear God, in the middle of the busy Christmas season, help me to pause and be still. Open my heart to the wonder of your presence and let me find peace in the quiet moments with you. Amen.

December 18th

You can discover the wonder of God's peace in the Nativity scene, which highlights that the Prince of Peace entered the world in humble surroundings.

Pursue Wonder:

Take time to look at a Nativity scene, in your home or elsewhere. Reflect on how the birth of Jesus in humble surroundings brings peace to your heart and the world.

Pray:
Dear God, thank you for the Prince of Peace who was born in humble surroundings to bring peace to the world. Help me to find peace in your presence and to share it with others. Amen.

December 19th

You can discover the wonder of God's joy and beauty in Christmas decorations.

Pursue Wonder:
Look at the Christmas decorations around you. Reflect on how they bring joy and beauty into your life, reminding you of the joy that Jesus' birth brings to the world.

Pray:
Dear God, thank you for the joy and beauty of the Christmas season. Help me to experience wonder whenever I see Christmas decorations and think of the awe-inspiring reality they celebrate – that you came to save me and be with me personally. Amen.

December 20th

Christmas fills the world with the hope of God's promises fulfilled through Jesus.

Pursue Wonder:

As you reflect on the first Christmas, you can discover the wonder of hope that brings peace to your heart and strength to your soul. Today, think about an area of your life where you need hope. Surrender it to God in prayer, trusting that God will faithfully fulfill his promises to you. As you do, let the wonder of God's hope fill you with joy and confidence in the future.

Pray:

Dear God, thank you for the hope you bring through Jesus. As I reflect on Jesus' birth, fill me with the wonder of your promises and the joy of knowing that you are always working for my good. Amen.

December 21st

On the longest night of the year, God's love is the light that shines in the darkness to guide you through the winter solstice.

Pursue Wonder:

As winter begins, embrace the darkness of the longest night. Reflect on how God's love shines brightly even in the darkest times, guiding you through life's winters.

Pray:

Dear God, thank you for the light of your love that shines even in the darkest times. Help me to trust in your presence through the long nights and to find comfort in your unending love. Amen.

December 22nd

God's strength is like the sturdy branches of a Christmas tree, holding up the weight of ornaments that tell the story of your life.

Pursue Wonder:
　As you hang ornaments on your Christmas tree, reflect on how each one tells a story. Consider how God's strength has supported you through all the moments of your life. Thank God for how he has supported you recently in an important way.

Pray:
　Dear God, thank you for the strength that holds me up through all the seasons of my life. Help me to see your presence in the stories of my past and to trust in your support for the future. Amen.

December 23rd

Family holiday traditions can become opportunities to experience God's wonder as you reflect on the joy and love God has brought to your family.

Pursue Wonder:
　This year, focus on one family tradition that brings you joy, such

as baking Christmas cookies together, reading the story of Jesus' birth out loud from the Bible, driving around to look at Christmas lights, or something else. As you participate, thank God for the gift of your loving family members (including close friends who are part of your family by choice) and the wonder of the memories you're creating.

Pray:
Dear God, thank you for the family traditions that make Christmas special. Help me to see the wonder of your love in these moments, and remind me of the joy that comes from being surrounded by loving family members. Amen.

December 24th

On Christmas Eve, God's wondrous love is revealed in the birth of Jesus, the Savior who came to bring light to the world.

Pursue Wonder:
Christmas is a time to express gratitude for the greatest gift of all – Jesus. As you reflect on the wonder of Jesus birth, let your heart overflow with thankfulness for the incredible love God has shown through his Son. Celebrate Christmas Eve by reflecting on the birth of Jesus at a church worship service. Consider how Jesus coming into the world is the ultimate expression of God's love, bringing light and hope to all. Spend time in prayer today thanking God for the gift of Jesus and the ways that a relationship with Jesus has brought positive change to your life. As you express gratitude, you'll experience more of the wonder of God's love during this season.

Pray:

Dear God, thank you for the gift of Jesus, who came to bring light to the world. I'm filled with wonder and gratitude for the love you have shown through my relationship with Jesus. Help me to live each day in thankfulness for this incredible gift, and to share that Jesus' love with others. Amen.

December 25th

Christmas reminds you that God came near to humanity in the form of a baby – Emmanuel, "God with us" – and that powerful truth inspires awe.

Pursue Wonder:

God cares deeply about your life and is always present. Spend time reflecting on the name "Emmanuel" today. How has God been present in your life recently? Thank God for being near to you, especially in times when you've needed his comfort and guidance. Let this truth fill you with wonder and peace this Christmas season.

Pray:

Dear God, thank you for coming to be with us through Jesus. I am in awe of you and grateful for your constant presence in my life. Help me to experience your wonder today as I reflect on the name Emmanuel. Amen.

December 26th

Stargazing in the clear winter sky can show you the wonder of God's creative glory.

Pursue Wonder:

Go stargazing this evening, despite the cold, to look at the wondrous stars in the winter sky. Let the glorious display inspire you with awe as you consider how God designed this vast universe so well and included you in it.

Pray:

Dear God, thank you for including me as part of your wonderful creation, and for loving me personally even though I'm just one small part of your vast universe. Amen.

December 27th

Gratitude in prayer opens your heart to seeing God's wonder in all circumstances.

Pursue Wonder:

As you pray today, focus solely on giving thanks. List every blessing you can think of – both large and small – in the time you have. Notice how gratitude shifts your perspective and helps you recognize God's wonder at work all around you.

Pray:

Dear God, thank you for your endless blessings. May my heart overflow with gratitude, and may I never take for granted the wonder of your goodness in my life. Amen.

December 28th

Focusing on God's promises in the Bible can fill you with awe at how God is always working for your good, even in unseen ways.

Pursue Wonder:
    Choose a promise from the Bible that speaks to you today. As you meditate on that promise, pray for the faith to trust in God's Word completely. Let the wonder of God's faithfulness fill your heart with hope and confidence.

Pray:
    Dear God, I'm relying on your promises today. Help me trust you and be reminded of your great love and faithfulness. May your promises fill my heart with peace and wonder. Thank you, faithful God. Amen.

December 29th

By reflecting on the past year, you can see glimpses of God's work guiding you forward.

Pursue Wonder:
    As the year comes to a close, reflect on the past year. Consider

how God has guided you through each moment, filling your heart with joy and gratitude.

Pray:
Dear God, thank you for guiding me through the past year with your loving wisdom. Help me to see your presence in every moment and to move forward with joy and gratitude. Amen.

December 30th

God's strength is your foundation as you prepare to step into a new year, trusting in God's guidance for the future.

Pursue Wonder:
Prepare your heart for the new year by reflecting on how God's strength has been your foundation this past year. Trust in God's guidance as you step into the future.

Pray:
Dear God, thank you for being my foundation this past year. Help me to trust in your strength and guidance as I step into the new year, ready to follow wherever you lead. Amen.

December 31st

On New Year's Eve, God's love is your companion, leading you from the old into the new with hope and confidence.

Pursue Wonder:

As you say goodbye to the old year and welcome the new, reflect on how God's love has been with you every step of the way. Let God's love give you hope and confidence for the year ahead.

Pray:

Dear God, thank you for your constant love that has guided me through this year. Help me to step into the new year with hope and confidence, trusting in your constant love. Amen.

ABOUT THE AUTHOR

Whitney Hopler is the author of the *Wake Up to Wonder* book from Elk Lake Publishing, Inc., and the Wake Up to Wonder blog at https://www.whitneyhopler.com/. Both help people thrive through experiencing awe. Whitney writes devotionals and articles regularly for Salem Media Group channels such as Crosswalk.com. She leads the communications work at George Mason University's Center for the Advancement of Well-Being. Whitney has served as a writer, editor, and website developer for leading media organizations, including Crosswalk.com, The Salvation Army USA's national publications, and Dotdash.com (where she produced a popular channel on angels and miracles). She has also written other books, such as the young adult novel *Dream Factory* and the nonfiction book *A Creative Life: God's Design for You*.

Made in United States
North Haven, CT
30 March 2025